The
Decal

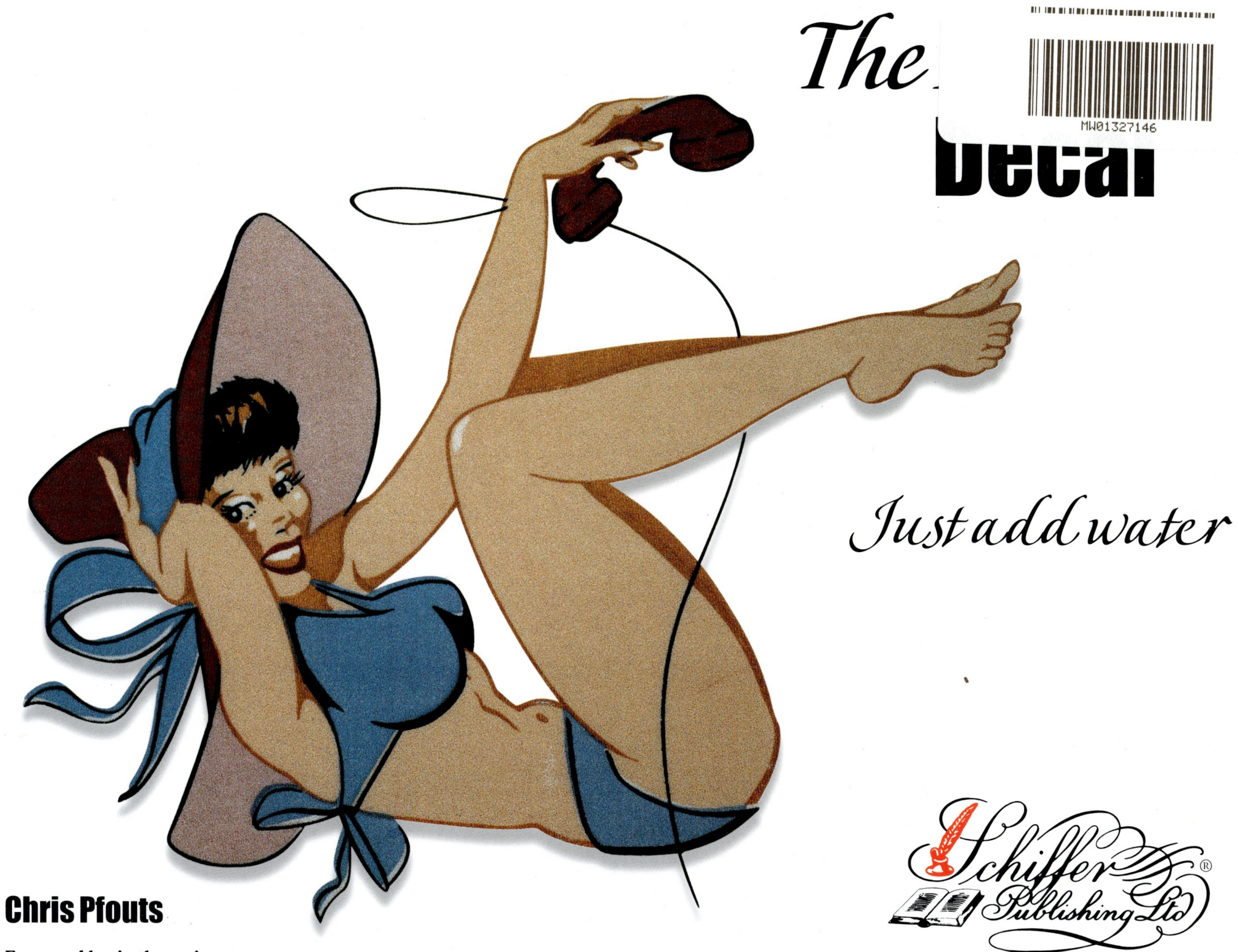

Just add water

Chris Pfouts

Foreword by Anthony Ausgang

Schiffer Publishing Ltd®

4880 Lower Valley Road, Atglen, PA 19310 USA

Library of Congress Control Number: 2001098925

Designed by Bonnie M. Hensley
Cover design by Bruce M. Waters
Type set in Impact/Souvenir Lt BT

ISBN: 0-7643-1541-2
Printed in China
1 2 3 4

In memory of my father, John Pfouts.

Published by Schiffer Publishing Ltd.
4880 Lower Valley Road
Atglen, PA 19310
Phone: (610) 593-1777; Fax: (610) 593-2002
E-mail: Schifferbk@aol.com
Please visit our web site catalog at **www.schifferbooks.com**
We are always looking for people to write books on new and related subjects. If you have an idea for a book, please contact us at the above address.

This book may be purchased from the publisher.
Include $3.95 for shipping. Please try your bookstore first.
You may write for a free catalog.

In Europe, Schiffer books are distributed by
Bushwood Books
6 Marksbury Ave. Kew Gardens
Surrey TW9 4JF England
Phone: 44 (0)20 8392-8585; Fax: 44 (0)20 8392-9876
E-mail: Bushwd@aol.com
Free postage in the UK. Europe: air mail at cost.
Please try your bookstore first.

Contents

Acknowledgments

For aiding and abetting this effort in so many ways, I am deeply grateful to John, Helen and Caroline Pfouts, Anthony Ausgang, Roger Bloomfield, Doug Nason, Jack Brink of Metal Form Products Co., Robin Mahaffey, Stanley Mouse, Kelton McMullen, Chet and Cheryl Crill, David J. Sale, Furry Couch, Paul Bearer, Von Franco, Don and Carol Illner, Dr. Elizabeth Tuttle (truly without whom this might still be a good intention), Steve Bonge, Debbie Ullman, Dave Cruse and Megan Mills, Brian Young, Big Ching, Utah Tom, Sherri Cullison, and Knuckles. Thanks to Steve Earle for the music.

Made by Meyercord, this was a cereal premium from Kellogg's in the 1950s. 2.5" x 4". $5-$7.

Foreword

In the early 1970s, my father dragged me away from my Lego blocks and took me to hot rod shows. I quickly became a custom car fanatic and soon began collecting any scaled-down versions of the creations I had seen. Before long I was making 1/24 scale model cars on the kitchen table while laughing at the neighbor's kid who made monsters. I pitied him because I had decals with my kits and he did not. I got to use the magic. I would watch anxiously as the decals separated from the paper in a dish of water, mentally trying to hurry up a process that demanded ulitmate patience. The application of decals to the finished car model was incredibly important: an off-kilter or split decal would render the whole thing utterly worthless. The amount of time one had to put the decal into position was frighteningly short; although I had never heard of Zen, I became one with the decal. In later years, as I switched interest from car models to fashion models, I realized that there had always been something inherently sexy about all that wetness and sliding, I just hadn't known it at the time.

When I got my first car, a 1970 Hornet, I had no money to hotrod it so I did the next best thing: I put on decals. Sure, I didn't have performance headers and I wasn't going to party down at the University of Texas but who knew? I sputtered around town showing off and that was enough. As I plied the junkyards looking for parts, I found that other drivers had done the same: there was no way that Nash had made it to both Carlsbad Caverns and New York City. Once I spent several hours trying to take out a car window that had a rare Roth decal on it. It was all show and no go.

I began collecting decals a few years ago and now they're kept in nice archival plastic pages. It's been years since I dipped any in water but maybe I'll do that tonight. Then put on Captain Beefheart's "Lick My Decals Off, Baby."

Anthony Ausgang
Los Angeles, 2001

Genuine classics of lowbrow humor in the decal format. In the 1960s, the screwed alligator was extremely popular as a T-shirt design. The guy flushing himself to end it all has been done in variations all sorts of places; as a three-dimensional figurine, as a T-shirt, on cocktail napkins, on tumblers, greeting cards. You name it, he's flushed himself there. A very popular gag in the 50s, he appeared less and less often in the 1960s. No maker's mark on either. Both 3" x 4". $5-$10 each.

Introduction

Until the late 1960s, waterslide decals were at least a small part of every American's life. They served as advertising signage; they told you what coins to stick in which slot, announced brand names, told people how to operate machines, presented safety warnings. They also offered the public a cheap, classy way to decorate almost anything. "Decals are not a fad," *Art Lac* magazine wrote in 1946. "They have become an essential part of our daily living."

True decals—waterslide decals—are an obsolete technology. They are kept alive today like other obsolete technologies—eight-track tapes, flathead engines, and muzzle loading guns—by hobbyists, restorers and collectors. But industry and mainstream society, which once lovingly embraced the decal, has forgotten them.

At the very heart of it, the function of decals was very basic: they were a way to put a printed image onto any object. It was as simple as that.

Simple but vital, especially to industry. Decals could carry any graphic, no matter how colorful or intricate. Anyone could put them on. They set quickly. They were inexpensive, and they looked great.

Waterslide decals are a thin film of lacquer coated on one side with adhesive. Before they are applied, the adhesive side is against the paper carrier. Soaking the decal in water loosens the adhesive from the paper backing. After it's applied, air dries the decal onto whatever its new host is. The decal becomes, effectively, a coat of lacquer. The final thickness is a miniscule one-thousandth (.001") to one and a half thousandths (.0015") of an inch—thinner, in many cases, than a coat of paint. By way of comparison, human hairs range between .002" and .004" thick.

Decals are tough, but they're also brittle—almost like glass. If handled roughly they chip and crack, but they don't peel. According to Jack Brink, a Southern California vending machine restorer and decal expert, the earliest decals were made with straight lacquer. When nitrocellulose lacquer—a more durable finish—became available in the early 1930s, decal makers quickly adopted it. Nitrocellulose lacquer remained as the chief component of decals, and it's still the most desirable choice for restorers who are trying to faithfully reproduce original equipment. (Modern environmental laws have made the use of any lacquer—where it can be used at all—an extremely touchy and expensive proposition. So far, at least in the decal world, no substitute has been found that's really its equal.)

Vintage decals were usually silk screened, which accounts for their rich colors and solid blacks. Once in place they were waterproof, and climatic conditions, from brutal sun and arid desert heat to bitter cold, did not affect them. If more protection was needed, decals could be coated with varnish or clear lacquer. Evidence of their durability in service is abundant. Anyone with experience in antiques has seen some readable remnant of an ancient decal still attached to an object that has been worn, savagely used, and left out in the weather. During World War II, decals carried almost all on-site equipment instructions. Waterslide decals were very good at what they did.

But vinyl records were very good at carrying music, and they are also obsolete. What happened to the waterslide decal?

Modern adhesives and plastics—in the form of self-adhesive stickers—were the main culprits responsible for the demise of the decal. As simple as it is to soak a decal in water for a few minutes and ease it into place, it's simpler still to peel the backing paper off a sticker and spank it onto whatever needs labeling. Before they are applied, decals are vulnerable to creasing (they crack and break if folded), and moisture is disastrous. A little crease does not affect a plastic sticker, and moisture is irrelevant.

Where the sticker loses out is in aesthetics. Decals are thin and elegant, and self-adhesive stickers are thick and ugly. A decal with clear space can really fool the eye; Fender Guitars have used decals for their tuning-head logos since day one, and they still do. With the clear coat sprayed on, the Fender lettering looks flawless against the natural wood, and you can't tell where the decal begins or ends. By comparison, a similar lettered sticker on clear plastic looks like a graphic maxi-pad. Stickers reek of cheap. Of course, if the product is roto-tillers and you want to advise folk to keep their fingers away from whirling parts, a sticker does fine.

The last big blow to the decal came from changing tastes in home decoration. In the middle of the 20th century, America was a very different nation. Household products were built to last. People bought an ice chest or a spice rack and expected to have the same ice chest and spice rack 20 years down the line.

Not everyone was able or motivated toward home improvement, but many people were, and doing it yourself—especially around the house—was the way they lived. Adults in the 1950s had been children during the Great Depression, and it left a mark of frugality and self-reliance on them. This combination of sturdy, permanent possessions and handyman spirit put a lot of people into a decorating mood. They wanted something beyond just a coat of fresh paint, and decals fit the bill. In the 1950s, adding a couple of big decal roses or angelfish to a clothing hamper was a common way to really put some sparkle in the bathroom.

Huge quantities of decals were targeted to the home-decoration market—little cute lambs, ivy vines, red poppies, and fat cartoon chefs all found a place in the kitchens and playrooms of America. Pink elephants jazzed up home bars and rumpus rooms. It's a decorating style that faded out about the same time as tailfins on cars, and it has not resurfaced.

In this book, there are very few home decorating decals. Artwise, they have nothing to offer that couldn't be found in a seed catalog, coloring book, or menu from the same period. On the collector front, hardly anyone cares. Heaps of virgin sheets showing cartoon tomatoes or photo-realistic vines are offered for sale all over the country. Online auctions are full of them, and there are almost no buyers. That art didn't endure and isn't worth resurrecting for a second look.

But there are plenty of decals with art that did endure, which is what this book is all about. Some feature image and design work that was as slick and innovative in its day as anything on the planet. Artists as famous as Alberto Vargas designed decals. And many of these images are unavailable in any other form.

Decals are an area of American industrial folk art that has been overlooked for far too long. Waterslide decals presented little scraps of art, orphan images with terrific appeal but no great meaning and no other home. The nature of the decal allowed people to put these scraps of art where they felt they would do the most good. This book is not meant in any way to be a comprehensive guide, but an overview of this under-appreciated and nearly forgotten little corner of the art market.

History

The word decal is a shortened version of "decalcomania," which comes from a French root meaning "to transfer a tracing." The "mania" suffix is hung on there to signify great enthusiasm.

Over the last 200 years, more or less, the word "decal" has been used as an umbrella term to cover any kind of transferable image on paper. Not many historians even mention decals. The few who did have been confused by the many dissimilar items that share the name.

Its oldest usage comes from Germany in the early 1800s, where a dry process called decal was developed to decorate ceramics. Early paper-based dry transfers were applied either under or over the glaze, and used on both ceramics and enameled products.

It was a major aesthetic breakthrough. Prior to their development, most chinaware and other ceramics were sold with no decoration at all. The only way to liven the pieces up was through hand painting, a process so slow and expensive that it kept decorated dishes out of the hands of all but the extremely wealthy.

Dry transfers meant that the middle class could finally eat from decorated dishes. The process quickly spread to England, Holland, and other hubs of 19th century ceramics production.

Today, the word decal is almost always used incorrectly. People say decal when they're talking about adhesive-backed vinyl stickers, the paper luggage stickers that graced steamer trunks in the opening half of the 1900s, or the wet-and-press temporary tattoos that children use for amusement.

The only true decals are the waterslide varieties. Ceramic waterslide transfers—printed with mineral colors and kiln-fired into place—are still in wide use on chinaware. Like household decorating decals, they aren't included in this book.

The first waterslide decals commercially produced in the United States (and not intended for kiln firing on ceramics) were made by Thomas Burke of Philadelphia in 1890. They were used to decorate bicycles, sewing machines, buggies and so on. Busy gingerbread trim was the style of the day, and decals made it easy. Burke's National Decalcomania Company prospered and was incorporated in 1922.

By the 1950s, three companies had come to dominate the decal world: Meyercord, Impko, and Duro.

Meyercord

Located in Chicago, Meyercord sold literally thousands of home decorating designs. The art was outstanding, as that stuff goes, and the quality of the decals was superb. Along with the florals and teddy bears, Meyercord offered a terrific line of girlie images, and it was Meyercord that introduced the famous "Double Face" drinking-glass pin-up decals—girls that were clothed on the outside and nude on the inside.

Duro Decals

Duro Decals, a smaller Chicago manufacturer, covered pretty much the same home-decorating ground as Meyercord. Between the two, American homemakers were well provided with cutesy windmills, fish, tulips, and cartoon circus wagons. Duro also made significant contributions in the girlie area.

A variety of Indian efforts. The painterly canoe and squaw and the mohawked fisherman with the mermaid are the only two not made by Impko. The mermaid decal is something of a puzzler—the artist went well out of his way to make the fisherman an Indian, but why? The painterly decals are scraps from a larger sheet, and have about zero punch as images. Their value is around a dollar as is, and wouldn't be much higher as a complete sheet. They were meant as home decorating decals, to brighten up a clothes hamper or chest of drawers. The rest are all worth $5-$10.

Impko

The other towering decal giant was Imprint Arts Products of Hackensack, New Jersey, better known as Impko. Impko stayed out of the over saturated cornball home decorating field. Instead, they focused on the youth market, the tourist, and the young automotive customizer. Impko was the Roger Corman of decals. They jumped on fads and trends, and they would release almost any image, no matter how strange—just throw it out there and hope it found an audience. They offered gags, hotrod and girlie images, souvenirs, monsters, and hundreds of cool designs that defy categorization. Their pool of art talent—whose names are sadly lost today in undeserved anonymity—really delivered quality. Some Impko designs caught the wild beatnik flavor of the fifties, and others displayed a sophistication far above what the subject matter really called for. Whether Impko's management was visionary or just lucky, they produced some genuinely timeless designs. And in the teenage and hotrod markets, they had almost zero competition.

Impko's main competition in the souvenir and travel field came from Lindgren-Turner of Spokane, Washington, and Baxter Lane of Amarillo, Texas. All three companies turned out quality decals with top-flight art.

Here, in the 21st century, waterslide decals are alive and well in the restoration and hobby communities. And there are more vintage decal collectors than ever.

Obsolete technology, yes. Dead? Hell no.

938

The beautiful realistic poppy and roses are examples of the kinds of florals sold for home decoration in the late 1940s and early 1950s. Decals of this kind are abundant in the marketplace today. The Meyercord and Duro flyers show suggested uses for decals in the home; Duro was another big source for home decorating decals. The poppies are about life size, measuring 4" x 6". The roses are about 6.5" x 8.5". $3-$5.

Beauty! Color! Charm!
IN HOME DECORATION

WITH MEYERCORD DECALS

Follow the mode set by leading interior decorators. Use Meyercord DECALS for decoration of kitchen, bathroom, nursery walls and accessories. You can choose from hundreds of DECAL designs, planned for all color schemes and produced in all sizes. You can be sure of finding the exact design, in the right size and in the correct coloring that will give added color, charm, and beauty to your room.

ONLY TWO MINUTES NEEDED TO APPLY A DECAL

3 EASY STEPS

1. Dip DECAL in WARM water for fifteen seconds. Remove from water and set DECAL aside for about one minute.
2. Slide design off backing paper FACE UP onto surface to be decorated. (See photograph.)
3. Smooth design down with cloth and allow to dry.

EASY TO APPLY. . ALL YOU USE IS WATER
THE MEYERCORD CO. · CHICAGO

FOR KITCHEN

FOR BATHROOM

FOR ACCESSORIES

These were bought in 1987 from an Impko card that was still hanging in a North Carolina gas station—one of those gas stations that keeps its displays until they're empty, no matter how many generations that takes, or how thick the fly poop gets. They were bought entirely on the basis of their staggering ugliness. The Flower Power decal has to be Impko's art nadir. This was a company that kept right on top of the teenage pulse in the 1950s, with slick images that hit the mark dead on. The media-driven Summer of Love was 1967, and the Flower Power decal probably came after that. It's an indication that Impko just didn't care any more. Ugly kitsch value brings these hideous items into the $5-$8 range.

Hillbilly humor is still making money for people in the eastern half of the United States. Gags like "Hillbilly Bubble Bath" (a plastic bag of beans with instructions to eat the beans an hour before getting into the tub) still sell well. Cartoonist Al Capp made a lifetime career out of the hillbilly humor of Dogpatch. These two Dogpatchers, Hairless Joe and Lonesome Polecat, only had one mission in life: making Kickapoo Joy Juice, a deadly potent drink that was liable to contain anything. If a batch needed body, for example, they threw one in. As with other Al Capp decals, value is $15-$20. The other hillbilly was probably sold as a travel or souvenir decal throughout West Virginia, Kentucky, and Tennessee. $5.

Gag decals, no maker's mark. It's hard to figure where the market was for these, but here they are. Most would have been better as postcards, and probably were available that way too. All 3" x 4" Each, $5.

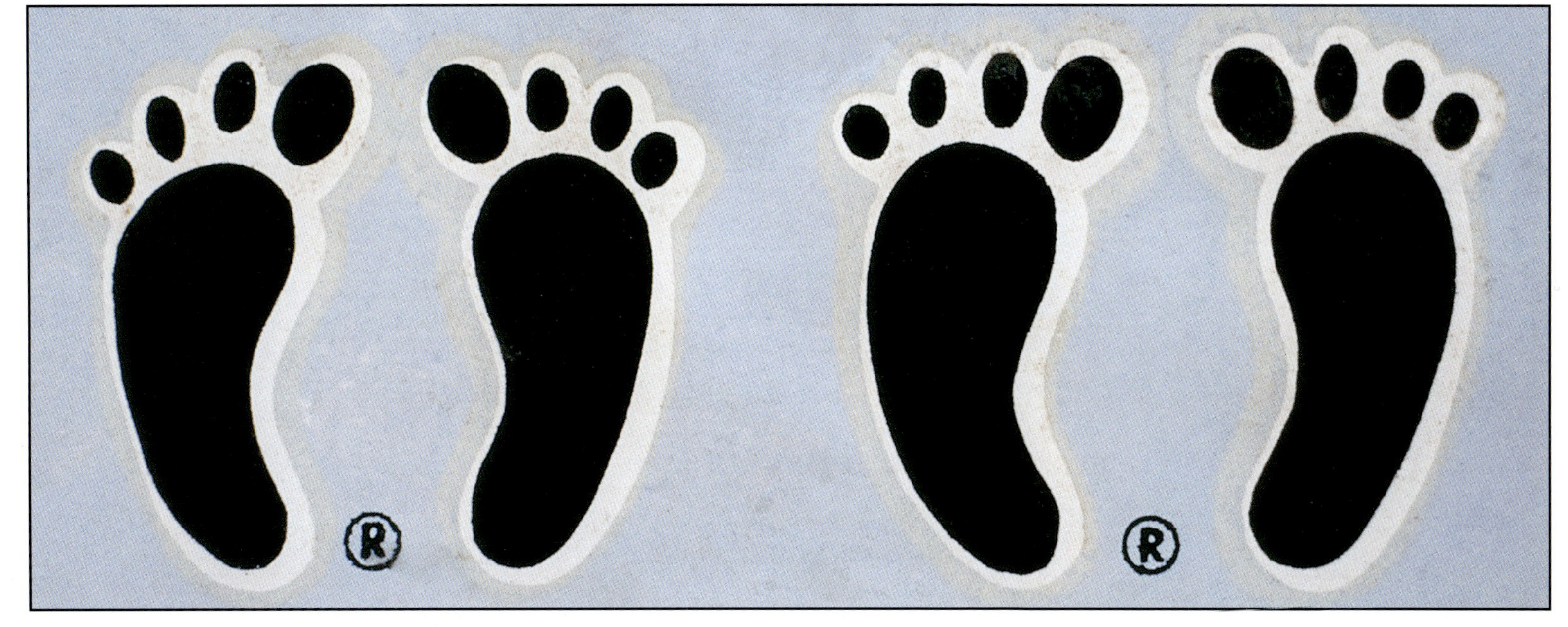

The bunny isn't exactly the logo from *Playboy*, but almost—close enough for government work, anyway. An immensely popular image, they were all over the place. They're still all over some places. Impko sheet, 10" long, $5-$10. The feet were the trademark of Eelco, a speed equipment manufacturer, but over time knock-offs were sold as "surfer feet." Bare foot prints became a trend through the 1960s. Stickers were sold so you could put life-size footprints on the wall, which was considered hilarious by many. Bumper to bumper over the top of Volkswagens was another common place for barefoot print stickers, also considered very funny at the time. And then there was the downward-pointing footprints between upward pointing footprints, a missionary sex position joke that took on a life of its own. Original Eelco decals go for around $10; knockoffs under $5.

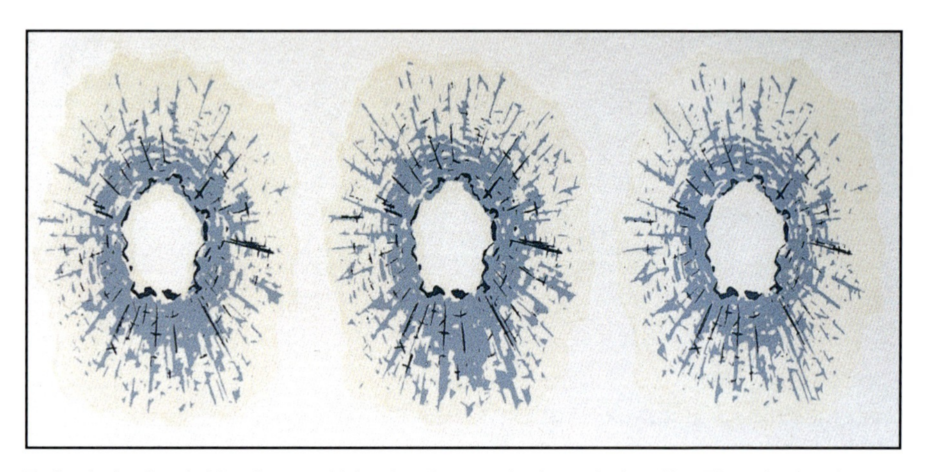

Bullet hole decals like these sold by the thousands through the 60s. The joke has been revived—truck stops are now selling extremely realistic bullet hole stickers intended for bodywork instead of glass. The new ones are so good you almost have to feel them to tell if the metal is bent in or not. The vintage decals are very common today, and a sheet like this is worth about $3.

Bombs away from Impko. This came on a sheet of two, not common. $10/pair.

Chapter 1

Travel & Souvenir

Travel and souvenir decals are widely collected today. Their main attraction, of course, is that they remind people of places they've been—which means they are still serving their original purpose.

In today's market most travel decals are relatively cheap and widely available. But there are expensive exceptions. Route 66 decals are highly prized. The more common (or boring, the two not necessarily being the same thing) designs from that legendary highway may only fetch a few dollars, but some varieties will set the collector back $50 or more. Amusement park decals, especially for famous attractions that have been lost to the wrecking balls of time, can also be quite expensive. A decal from Venice, California's lost and lamented Pacific Ocean Park brought around $75 in an online auction in 2001.

Decal manufacturers that worked the travel market found their meat and potatoes in the ordinary map-style souvenir decal. Most of these, even if they include some notable landmark image, will only bring about five bucks these days—and some of the duller varieties will not even pull that.

Travel decals with girlie art, on the other hand, are highly desirable, and offer terrific graphics. There are several series of girlie travel decals, none carrying a manufacturer's name. The "Miss America" decals had sophisticated airbrushed gals and always included a state outline in red. Another series had a red heart with each pin-up. A third series had a loose kind of pin-up art that has tons of character.

In the 50s and 60s, Buckeye Lake was a thriving central Ohio attraction. Two key elements here: a bikini girl and a roller coaster. $25.

A little rustic humor—even the mule seems to be enjoying itself. $10.

Parts of North Dakota also lay claim to Paul Bunyan. One thing is sure—a blue ox is not the kind of Babe best suited to travel decals. $7.

It was one of the grimmest of our federal prisons. Nonetheless, Alcatraz was always good for a laugh in the decal world. The 8-ball and chain was a nice touch. Alcatraz decals are semi-difficult to find these days. Either one, $15.

This rare piece was located in Bangkok, Thailand. The art and design are magnificent. The prop plane dates it from before commercial jetliners, but the slice of outer space in the background optimistically foreshadows things to come. It's not in useable condition, but it'd be a crime to fool with it anyway. $45 in this condition. If mint, $75-$100

Good art is good art—the author's favorite travel decal. $15.

This place looks as respectable as an all-night border town eatery could look, and it probably was. A lot of Mexican-border nightspots featured activities that might make you think twice about advertising yourself as a patron. Evidence of a visit to Tijuana's Blue Fox, for example, might make women insist on seeing a note from your doctor before agreeing to a date. Respectable though it may have been, Restaurant Gomez felt compelled to advertise "Genuine Liquors and Wines"—assurance that the stuff in your glass was really what the bottle said it was. Too bad it's such an ugly decal. $10.

This is what Mexican decal art should look like. If in new condition, $10.

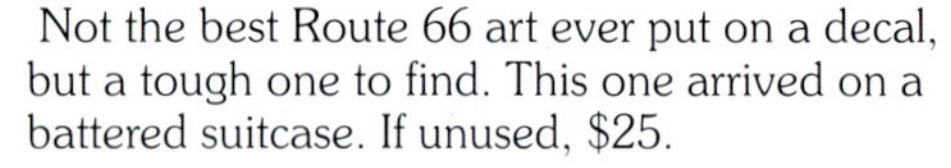

Not the best Route 66 art ever put on a decal, but a tough one to find. This one arrived on a battered suitcase. If unused, $25.

Extremely lame overall design, but it's kind of an eerie piece when you look closely. $5.

The arrow looks like it's pointing to California, but no clue what road they're referring to. Possibly Angeles Crest. There's some merit in its strangeness, but its no great shakes graphically. $10.

A souvenir of someone's visit to a gentlemen's club. Although it doesn't look it, this is indeed a waterslide decal, and probably one of the few ever made to advertise an ecdysiast watering hole. The art puts it firmly in the 70s or later, which makes the decal a strange choice of medium. $15.

Ugly and plain, or just plain ugly. With all the wild, colorful, and exotic/erotic pleasures to be found within the borders of Louisiana, "Old World Charm" and some bad menu art is the best they could do? Under $5.

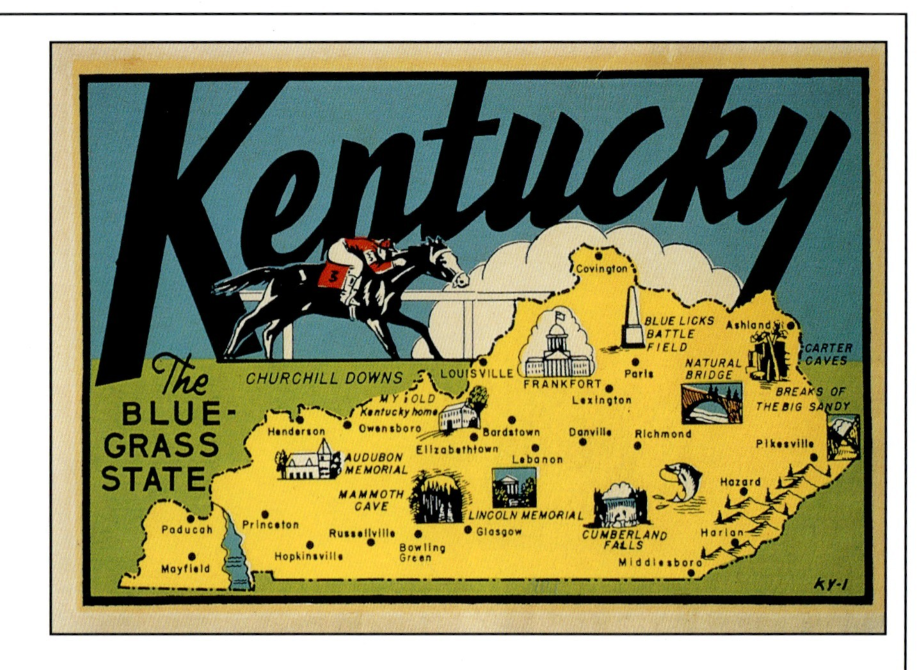

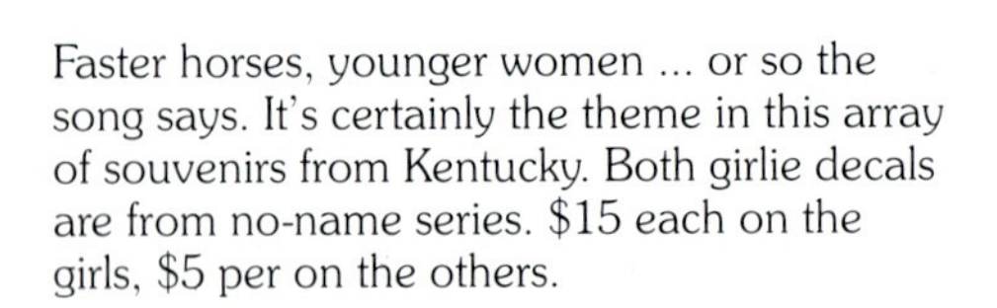
Faster horses, younger women ... or so the song says. It's certainly the theme in this array of souvenirs from Kentucky. Both girlie decals are from no-name series. $15 each on the girls, $5 per on the others.

Georgia's "Peach State" moniker made life easy for decal artists. "She's a peach," was common enough slang for a pretty girl that it could be slipped casually into the visual language. Each, $10.

Georgia travel decal from Baxter Lane, except the peaches here look more like lemons with butt cracks. Using the girl as half a frame was a bad design idea—it pulls your eye to the right and straight out of the picture. $8.

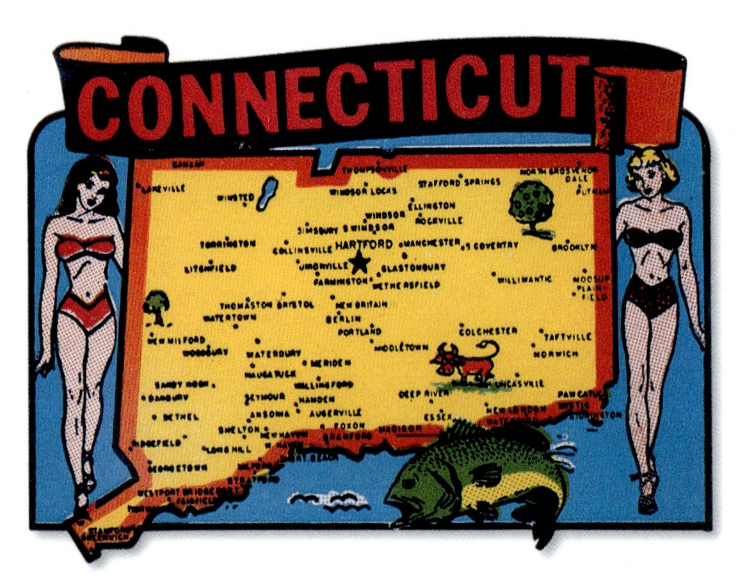

It's a sad commentary when insurance is the only state characteristic you can tack onto a picture of a pretty girl in a bathing suit. And despite a brace of bikini babes, the map decal is sunk in ugly. Girl, $15; map, $5.

The "Corn-Bred Charmer" is from the "Miss America" series. Something seems to have torn the bathing suit bottom nearly off the "Sweetheart of the Corn belt," but no indication of what it might have been. Either, $15.

A case when the girls in both series are equally appealing. The fur stole and miner's cap give "Miss America" a very inviting look. But the combination of moonshine whisky and a hillbilly doll is the stuff of dreams. Either, $15.

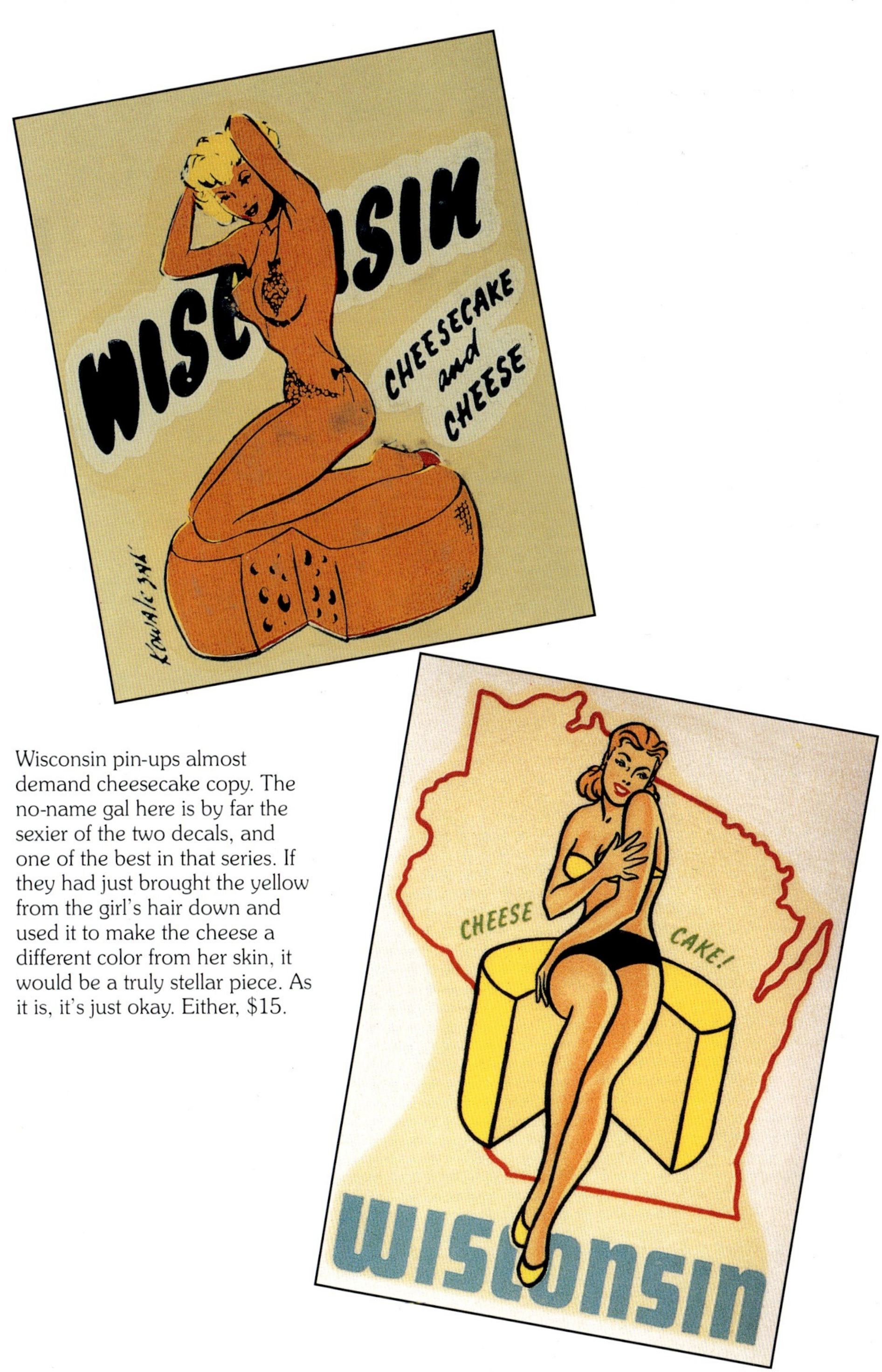

Wisconsin pin-ups almost demand cheesecake copy. The no-name gal here is by far the sexier of the two decals, and one of the best in that series. If they had just brought the yellow from the girl's hair down and used it to make the cheese a different color from her skin, it would be a truly stellar piece. As it is, it's just okay. Either, $15.

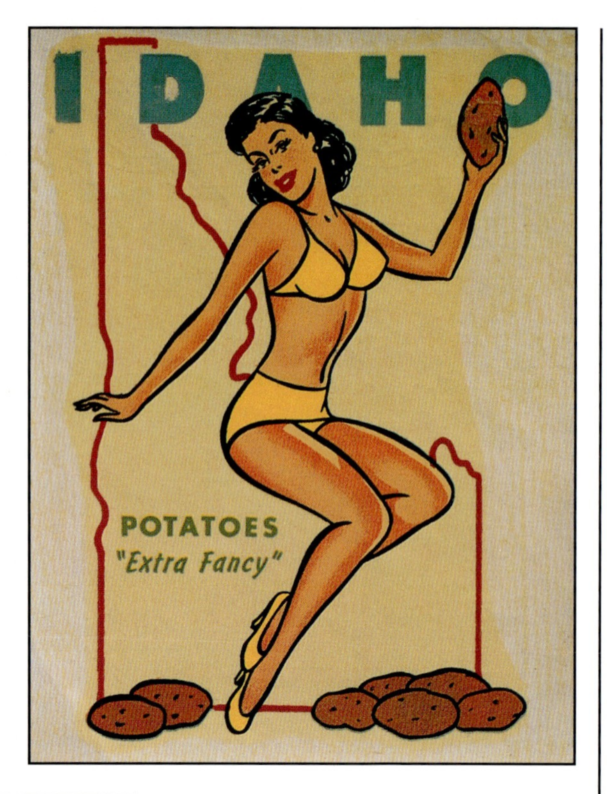

Quality art on the "Miss America" decal, as always. "Spud" is another story. There were quite a few of these anthropomorphic Idaho potato decals, and every last one of them looks fecal. The California Raisins had the same problem. Despite the fact that you want to push the chrome handle and flush ol' Spud, this decal will bring $10. This particular "Miss America" has a rip, but if mint, $15.

The "Gulfport Miss" is a great example of the busty, free-wheeling pin-up art found on Baxter Lane decals. Gulfport has long been a thriving vacation town on the Redneck Riviera, and this decal probably sold very well. Either, $15.

The mystery here is why "Miss Massachusetts" is pointing to a hankie. Or is that supposed to be a drooping diploma, or what? Neither of these pieces has a worthwhile hook. They'd have been better off with baked bean or Boston Tea Party gags. Either, $15.

Another mystery—why would her money go to Tennessee? Country records? Even though her mouth looks like a fresh wound, the "Charmin' Little Rebel" at least makes sense. Each, $15.

Although there were plenty of surfers in California by the 1950s, the sport hadn't yet spread to the frosty places you find it today, like England and Maine. Surf riders were still Hawaiian icons, as evocative of the islands as hula dancers and ukuleles. The return of the longboard to active duty has driven the value of all vintage surfing images straight up, lofting a mint surfer decal like this into the $25 range.

An Impko product, kind of busy design wise and not too attractive overall. If it wasn't Hawaii, it would only be worth about half of its $10 value.

The uke-playing Honolulu hula girl is a genuine high point in girlie travel art, and one of the finest examples of sexy decal graphics to ever come down the pike. Absolutely magnificent. $30.

This decal from Rainbow Rollerland is unusual because most skating rinks advertised on adhesive-backed paper stickers. It's not mint, but still worth $10.

"Miss Liberty Belle" is a tasty bit of pin-up art, while the gal with the lantern looks as if working on the railroad has driven her stark, staring insane. $15 each.

Both of these were picked up in a gift shop at Vegas' McCarran Airport in 1985, about 20 years after most souvenir decals had been replaced by stickers. That kind of dead stock is a real score. 50s art, judging by the style of the slot machine. Either one, $10.

The nautical flavor of Michigan's "Miss America" makes you want to go buy a boat and troll: $15. While the Belle Isle decal is creased, it still carries some nostalgia value: $5.

In any series some individual pieces are going to be better than others. The combination of fishnet stockings, the 3-D pose, and the sou'wester hat really makes the Maine "Miss America" stand out. $20.

Florida

Florida has been a vacation destination forever. It has 660-plus miles of beaches—not counting lakes and riversides—making bikini-clad females as much a part of the local landscape as convertibles. Over the years, alligators have also become visual symbols of the Sunshine State, along with synchronized water skiers and palm trees. It sure beats having your state summed up as the home of the insurance industry, like Connecticut.

A tasty deco-hangover late 40s look to this imaginative decal. Good color selections and clean design. $10.

Probably from the 1940s, these two unusual bordered decals were made by Bloom Brothers of Minneapolis. Eye-catching design and great, humorous art. Either, $15.

The two most basic souvenir elements, a girl and a map. Made by Impko, $8.

Baxter Lane's unmistakable pin-up style—crude but appealing all the same. Putting the state border in outline gives it a look vaguely similar to the "Miss America" series. $10.

Key West

Key West is literally the end of the road. US Highway 1 starts in Fort Kent, Maine and ends here, at the southernmost point in the United States. For a small town on a dead-end street, it's one busy tourist mecca.

These 14 Impko decals show the scattergun thinking that sometimes ruled the decal business. Just about the only Key West tourist activities not celebrated as a decal are watching the sunset at Mallory Dock and getting hammered on Duval Street.

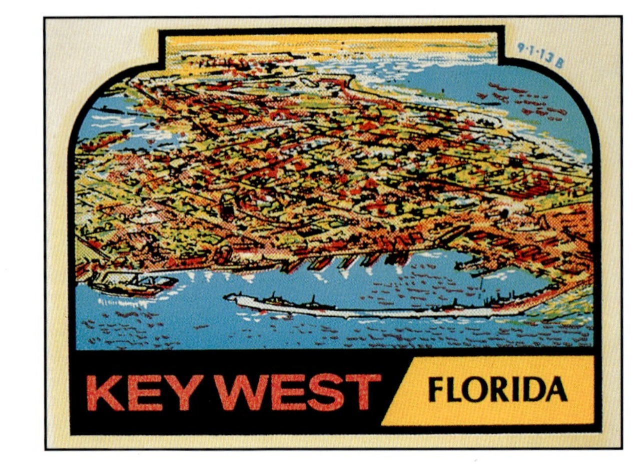

The collection is not quite as diverse as it first appears. Impko was masterful at reworking and recycling images. The scuba diver and sailfish are virtually the same decal, for example. And they share their mason-jar shape with the Hemmingway Home, Big George and the southernmost point. A number of the others share structural similarities. There are two identical pictures of the Overseas Highway presented in different color/ways. Both bathing beauty decals have the same girl, just a flopped image. The diving girl was a design that Impko sold all over the country, any place there was recreational water. The two girl decals, $10 each; the rest, $5 per.

No town in America owes as much to rock'n'roll as New Jersey's Asbury Park. The music of Bruce Springsteen put it on the map. But when this Impko decal was made, Asbury was just another Jersey shore town with a great boardwalk—a boardwalk that was recently made famous all over again by *The Sopranos*. The decal features the same diving girl as the two from Key West. $10.

New Mexico imagery often features cowboys and cactus. Two exceptions here. The Taos decal is on a vintage suitcase. The pin-up: $15.

Washington's "Miss America" is nearly as sexy as Maine's. There's something about a girl in a nurse's uniform. Miss Vermont still has a chunk of the glassine envelope glued to her. When this happens, combined with the age involved, the decals just self-destruct when dipped in water. Any of the girls in this series, in near-mint shape, are worth $15-20.

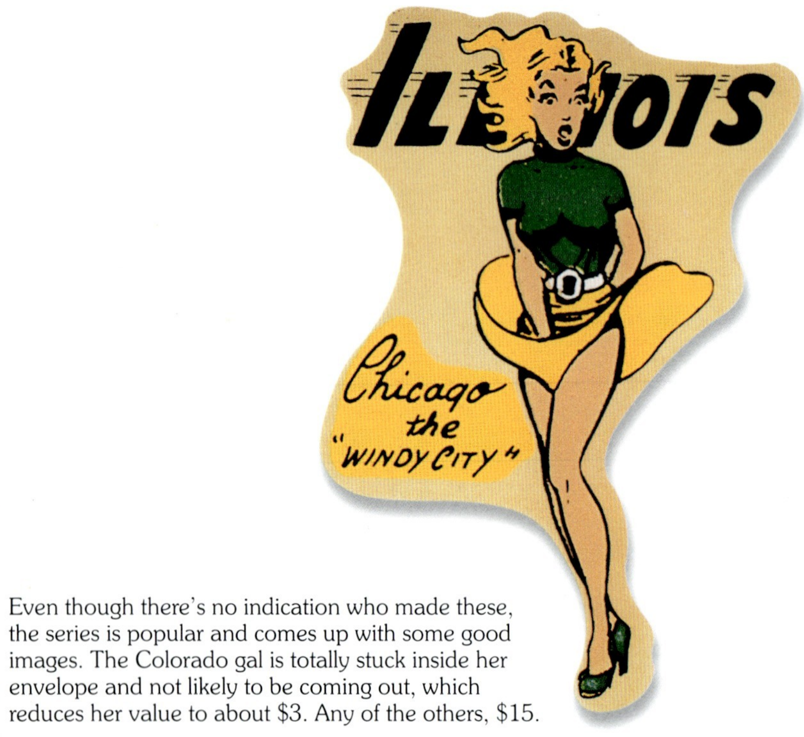

Even though there's no indication who made these, the series is popular and comes up with some good images. The Colorado gal is totally stuck inside her envelope and not likely to be coming out, which reduces her value to about $3. Any of the others, $15.

PIKE'S PEAK
or
BUST

WHAT'S THIS GOT TO DO WITH
THE PRICE OF WHEAT?

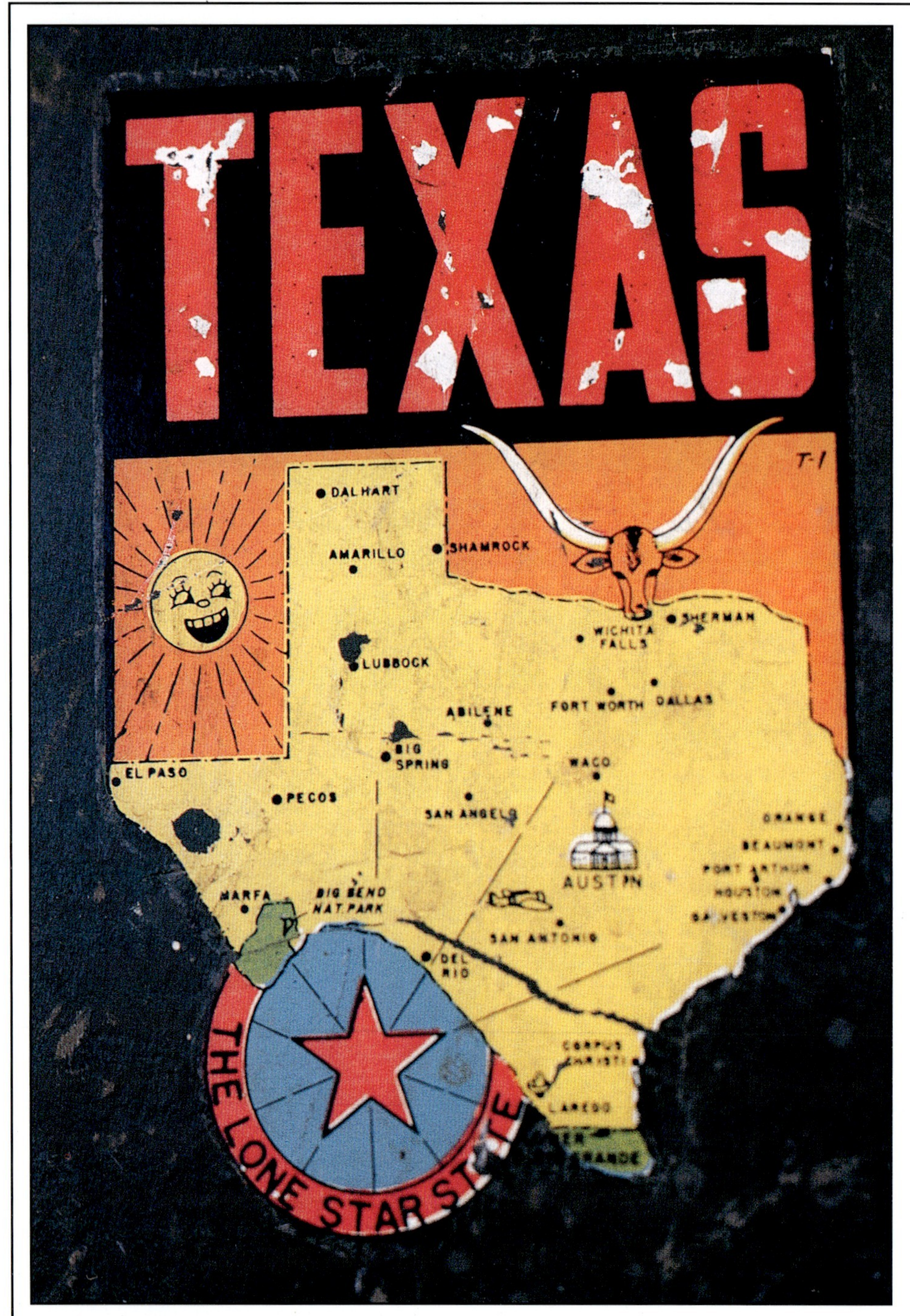

The map decal, stuck on a well-traveled suitcase, is about as dull as a souvenir decal can get. But when it comes to bull shipping, that's another story. $10.

Chapter 2

Girlie

Decals are a rich source of girlie art. Pin-up art is homegrown Americana. Girlie decals can wear the same crown. Some have messages, written or otherwise. Some have a humorous hook. Some are just pictures of women, riding on their good looks alone. It is, as they say, all good.

Charles G. Martignette, in his book *The Great American Pin-Up*, offers a useful definition: "A 'pin-up' image is one that shows a full-length view of its subject and characteristically has an element of a theme or some kind of story. The woman in a pin-up is usually dressed in a form-revealing outfit, either one that may be worn in public, such as a bathing suit, sun suit, or skimpy dress, or one that is more provocative and intimate, such as lingerie. Sometimes a pin-up may be shown as a nude, but this is more the exception than the rule." Among the names in the world of pin-up art, few are bigger than Alberto Vargas. One of the Impko decals in this section is signed by Vargas. A number of the others look similar, and are almost certainly his work.

Even though Vargas is the big name—indeed the only artist's name—on this grouping of girlie decals, his dames are by no means the sexiest in decaldom. Girlie decals range from magnificent to just plain strange, and Vargas' decal work falls right about in the middle.

Glamour Girl Series

This series is just pure, killer, pin-up art. They are numbered for inventory, but there is no maker's name on the back. Although we can fit the decals into categories, the manufacturer didn't bother. Any of the Glamour Girl Series decals will bring from $10 to $25, depending on the art and the condition.

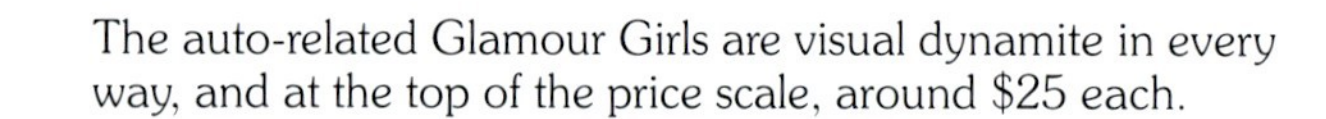
The auto-related Glamour Girls are visual dynamite in every way, and at the top of the price scale, around $25 each.

This is much better girlie art than is usually found around barware. "Hot Toddy" and "Maid in Manhattan" are great examples of the richness of color that could be brought to decals. Like the auto girls, these are at the top end of the value scale.

A series of gambling-related Glamour Girls only makes sense. After years of searching and collecting, though, this is the only one that has come to light. Art wise, it's not terrific, but the dice on her bra are a nice touch.

Miscellaneous Glamour Girls, and not a clinker in the bunch.

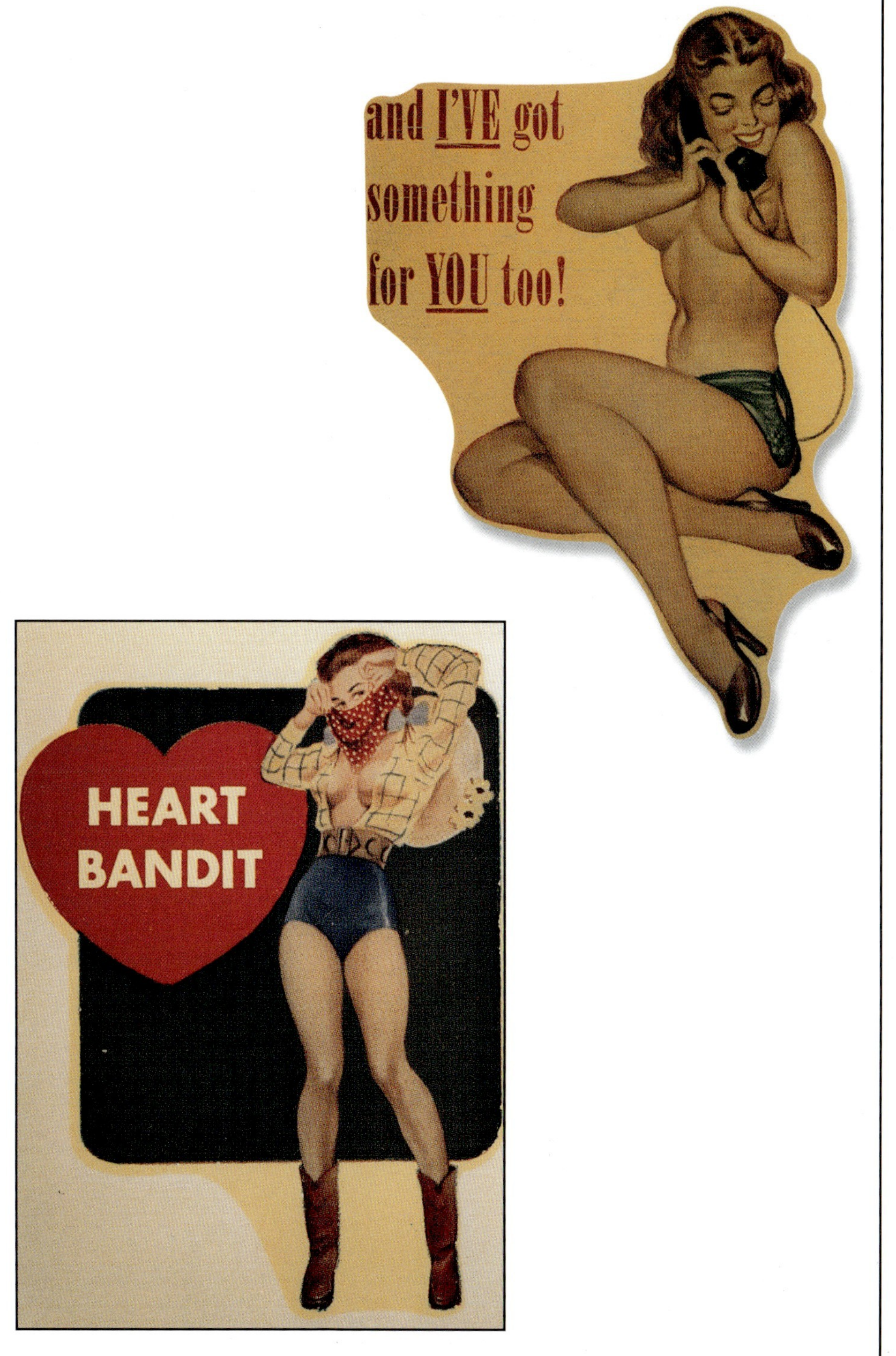

From the same maker, a solo entry from what they called the "Moral Builders" series. Surely it was meant to be Morale, since a nautical nymphet is hardly going to elevate anyone morals. But it won't plunge them into the depths of depravity either. $15.

A trio of sporty young gals from Meyercord—the very essence of All-American health and vigor. Each one is 6" tall, and the whole sheet measures 8.25" x 6.5". Entire sheet, $15.

Bathing suits, sun hats, and telephones held anywhere but to the ear. The girl in the red suit has a breast agreement problem—one is much larger and lower than the other. Absolutely no maker's name, not even instructions on the back—although all that information may have been cut away. Each measures around 3" x 4". The sheet remnant as is $12-$15.

There are a zillion variations of the nude silhouette with bubbles in the decal world. Duro sold an extensive line of them, including dancers, swimmers and mermaids. This one is from Meyercord, and measures 6.25" x 8.25". Prices vary with size and style.

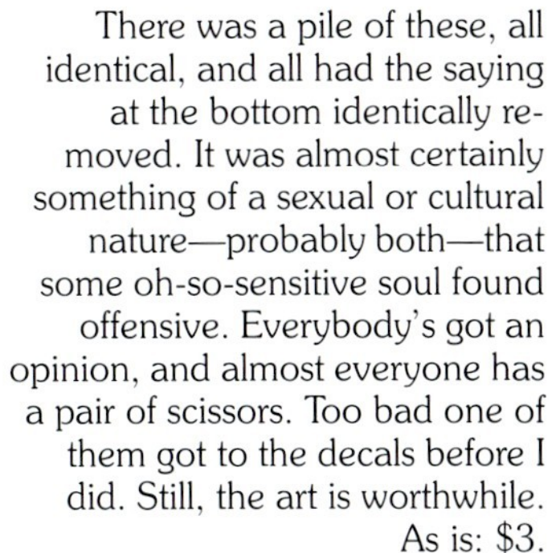

There was a pile of these, all identical, and all had the saying at the bottom identically removed. It was almost certainly something of a sexual or cultural nature—probably both—that some oh-so-sensitive soul found offensive. Everybody's got an opinion, and almost everyone has a pair of scissors. Too bad one of them got to the decals before I did. Still, the art is worthwhile. As is: $3.

Duro mermaid, perfect for any room with a beachcomber flavor. These too came in different sizes. This one measures approximately 6" x 8". $10.

No maker's name, but a very nice piece. Probably 1950s. $10-$15.

Meyercord beauties, probably late 1940s or early 1950s. A screaming retail deal at their original 10 cent price. Girls measure just under 6" tall. Either, $10.

Three fantastic Impko pin-ups aimed at merchants with a strongly male clientele. They were acquired in the 1980s, the very last of the vintage stock from a midtown Manhattan joke and novelty emporium. $20-$25 each.

Distaff diversity and a straight flush in spades. Impko. $10-15.

Packed with pulchritude and brimming with beauty, here are nine nifties for your decalling pleasure—equally divided between golden blondes, sultry brunettes and fiery redheads. The sheet is badly damaged and would disintegrate if placed in water, but that's a technical detail; the art suffers not. The Meyercord sheet measures about 8" x 6.5", and cost 25 cents when it was new. Today, if mint: $25-$35.

Today, the devil girl is a familiar image to millions; lust personified as a stacked, crimson temptress. Hot stuff, indeed. A Hollywood artist named Coop is responsible for her elevation as a current icon. This version by Impko is pretty tame by Coop's standards, but she's got beaucoup 50s charm all the same. 4" tall. $10-$15.

Making hoe jokes would be like shooting fish in a barrel. Another Meyercord all-American figure of vigor, roughly separated from her sheet sisters and creased in the process. An excellent image, but as a decal, she's only worth $2 in this condition.

A large (approx 11" x 14") sheet of pin-ups out of West Germany. The art is not even close to the level of the Meyercord group, but it's not hideous, either. Sheet, as is, $20.

Another Impko ingénue with a very similar look to the Vargas decal. $10.

The one signed Vargas decal. It was sold by Impko and the image measures 5" tall. This one is near mint, $15-$20.

Split card of bathing beauties from Impko—it's just plain great art. Near mint, $10-$15.

Another double-header of pin-ups from Impko. The problem with these two is the lack of a visual hook. Cute, but uninspiring. $10.

Looking at these two is like one of those "find-the-differences" puzzles that are so vexing to children. We'll save you the trouble: in one, the Indian girl has a plain yellow swimsuit—in the other decal the suit has a diamond pattern, and her headdress has changed color slightly. The other gal has a yellow and red striped swimsuit in one picture and a plain red suit in the other. Impko was big on recycling images when they could. Either of these, $10-$15/sheet.

A pair of beach-bound babes, complete with a towel. Impko. $15.

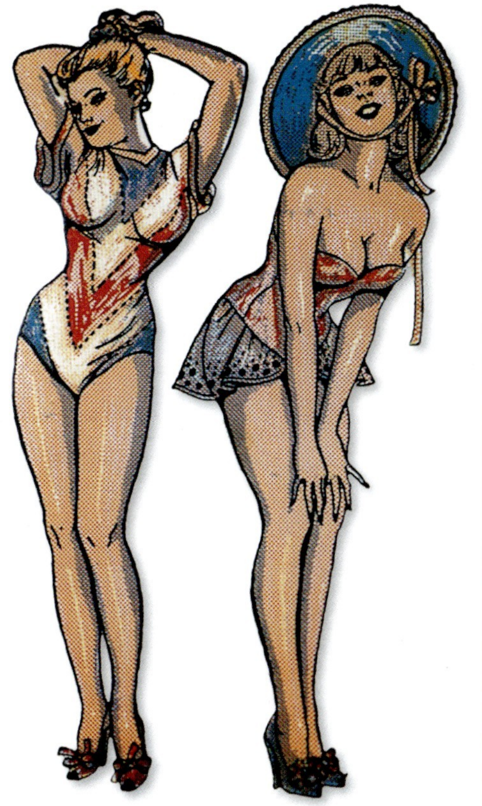

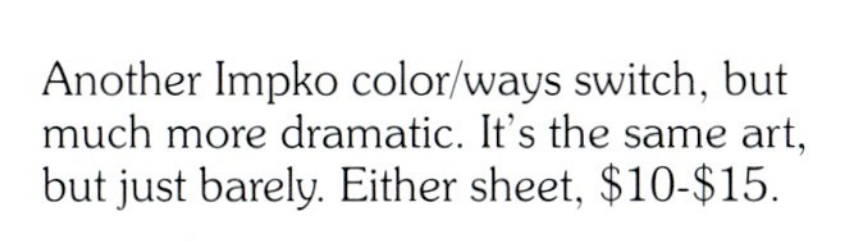

Another Impko color/ways switch, but much more dramatic. It's the same art, but just barely. Either sheet, $10-$15.

Three big barroom belles from Duro, all from the same sheet. Each is 8" tall, and the extra size just magnifies their artistic shortcomings. They're not just dull, these girls are actually anti-erotic. One is a nude in fishnet stockings riding an erectile-angle bottle, her butt peeking out from a modified French maid's skirt. From that description you'd expect to see absolute visual dynamite. After all, girls straddling tilted phallic objects—rockets, bullets, cannon barrels—are one of the hottest girlie genres known to man. Instead of a pin-up prize, Duro delivered a D.O.A. dud-o-roonie. Three of them. The sheet, if you could find a buyer, $15.

There's no mistaking the great look of a Baxter Lane pin-up. The gag is a solid gold classic, and there were other versions from other manufacturers. One had a dotted-line phantom brick shithouse drawn around a standing girl. $10-$15.

These timeless jokes about girls and their asses (usually tired asses or dragging asses) are more often found on postcards. They make fine decals, though. 1950s vintage, no maker's name. Either one, $5-$10.

GRRR
YORE
MAH MEAT!

AH'M WIF YO!

Al Capp, creator of the *Li'l Abner* comic strip, had powers far beyond those of mortal men when it came to drawing women. Breast for shapely breast, cheekbone for cheekbone, gam for well-turned gam, Al Capp was every bit as good as Elvgren, Mac Pherson, or Vargas—but in a cartoonier way. Some say he was better. Mastercraft Decalcomania Co. of Chicago issued the *Li'l Abner* series decals. The blonde is Daisy Mae, who eventually became Li'l Abner's wife. The brunette fighting off the Dogpatch-style wooing is Moonbeam McSwine. The guy trying to pitch the woo is a Scragg—member of a subhuman family that has hair on the bottoms of their feet. It is against the law for a Scragg to marry a human being, but they continue to try. The redhead lives with wolves, and shows up only peripherally in the strip. Any *Li'l Abner* series decal in near-mint condition, as these are, $20-$30.

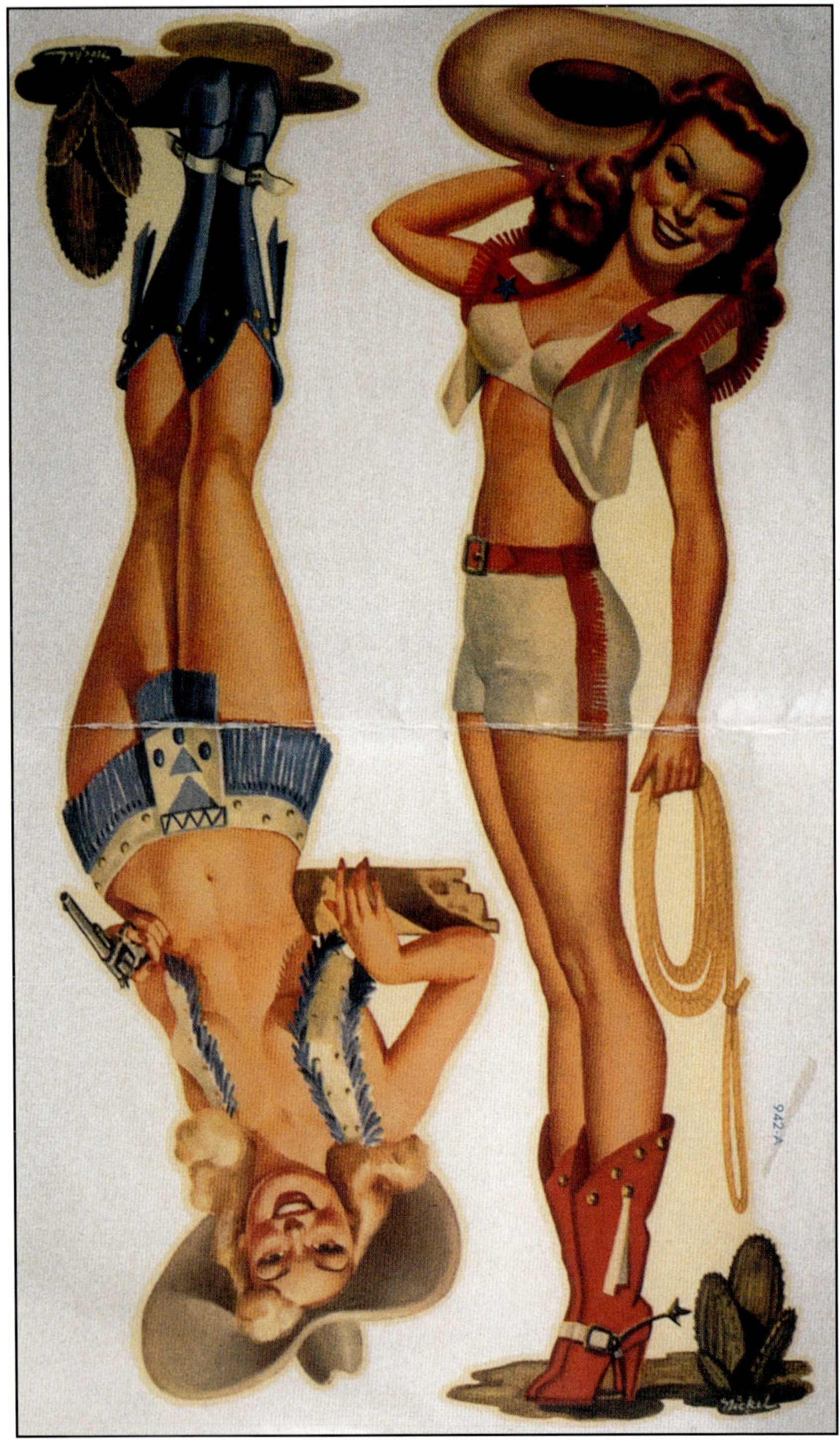

Size counts. These tall drinks of water measure a full 13" from their ten-gallon tops to their big bad boot heels. Made by Meyercord. This pair has been folded in the middle, but in mint condition a pair of these sagebrush sweethearts will bring $60 and up.

There's girlie decals and then there's this: light years ahead and miles above. Souvenirs of this caliber don't come along nearly often enough. Vintage hurricane glasses are semi-rare. For one thing, they're handed out to drunken tourists on a toot. Secondly, most are not what you'd classify as heirloom possessions. This one survived a night in the Quarter and many years in a Kentucky collection before the author got it. Value: Priceless.

Chapter 3

Lady Luck

Lady Luck is by far the best known and most enduring decal image ever. Nothing else even comes close.

The traditional Lady Luck is an exaggeratedly doe-eyed race-track queen with a horseshoe for a tiara. Displaying a monkey wrench in one hand and a shamrock in the other, and sporting dice earrings, 8-ball bra cups, and card suits on her tiny wrap-around skirt (with a strategically placed inverted spade at the junction), she is a child of the studio rather than the streets. At least, it appears that way. Lady Luck was copyrighted in 1941 by one Paul Benson. The design was sold as decals and felt jacket patches. When World War II pushed hot-roders into military gigs, Lady Luck came along and found herself gracing the nose of at least one US bomber.

The thirst for 50s icons has brought Lady Luck renewed fame. Sixty years after her introduction, she's more visible than ever, appearing on T-shirts, Zippo lighters, tattoos, enameled pins, as a sticker, in rock'n'roll art—all the usual suspect locations for a cool vintage graphic.

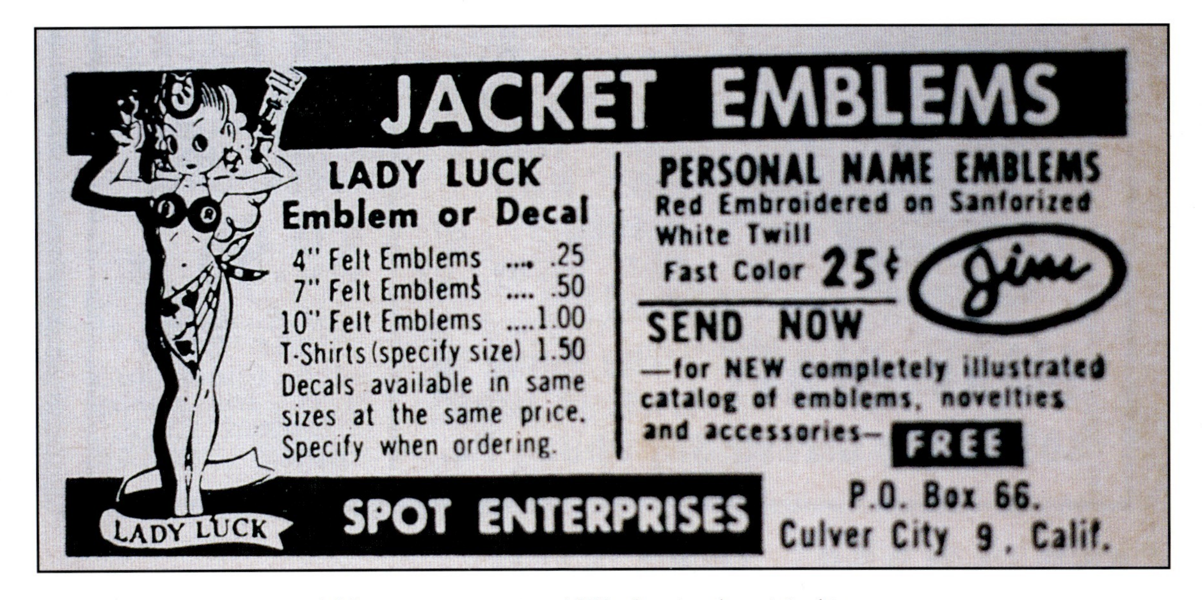

Ad from a car magazine, 1958, showing the original image.

This is as close to the 1941 classic as Impko got. They substituted a large black ball for the banner, and left the rest as it was. The small decal is 2" tall, the larger ones, 6" tall. Loose smalls, $5-$8 each; Two-sheet of larger decals, $20-$30.

Despite the history and tradition behind the classic Lady Luck, some people prefer this image. As a composition, the girl seated in the horseshoe looks great. Down in the mojo details, though, the addition of a wishbone and a rabbit's foot don't make up for the loss of the 8-balls. Even with the checkered flag it's not an even trade. The heart of it, though, is that the original stands completely alone as a design. There's nothing else like her. This one is a specially-flavored pin-up, which is not nearly as interesting. It's a large decal, about 8" tall and 5.5" wide. $30-$40.

Lady Luck meets Hot Head in a truly stunning piece of art. There are a few differences between the larger and smaller decals, in the flames and the eyes of the skull. The bigger version (measuring about 9" x 7") is as rare as hen's teeth and highly sought after. The smaller (3.5") decal: $10-$15. The big gun: $65-$80.

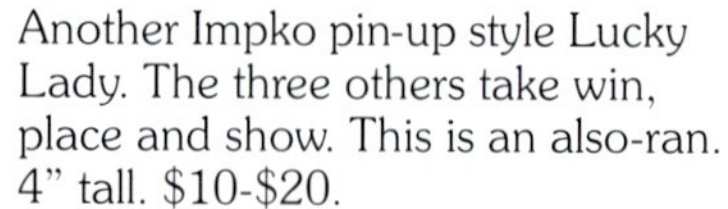

Another Impko pin-up style Lucky Lady. The three others take win, place and show. This is an also-ran. 4" tall. $10-$20.

Chapter 4

X-Ray Glasses

These are a kick. Tame by modern standards, in their day they were definitely an adult gag, and not something to share with the kiddies.

Although not all of these were made by Meyercord, it was the Chicago decal giant that brought them to the do-it-yourself market. Their "Double Face Cuties" cost 35 cents for a "surprise package" of six ethnically assorted dames.

"Cuties," the envelope says, "help your guests identify their glasses." That's a plausible enough excuse. Of course, letters or numbers would accomplish the same thing if your guests weren't smart enough to remember what they were guzzling: "Who's drinking Mai Tai letter G?"

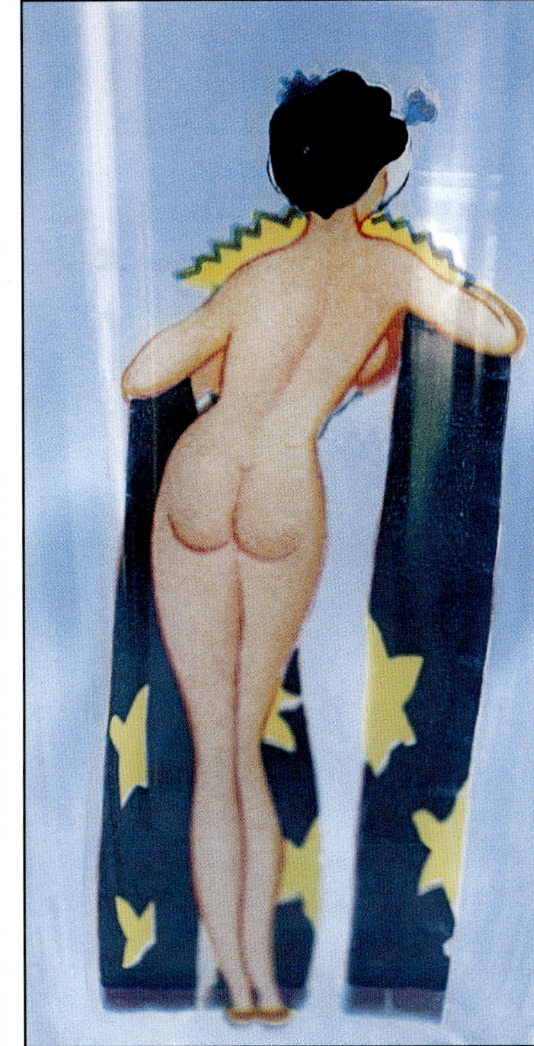

Exotic ingénue from the exciting Orient, complete with a star-spangled kimono; empty glass reveals nothing but air on her bare behind. $15-$25.

It's hard to picture any woman seriously exercising in a get-up like this, but it does provide a nice visual set-up for the bent-over cutaway view. $15-$25.

The hula girl is unusual because she offers a front view from inside the glass instead of a rear aspect. This came as part of a set, complete with decalled pitcher. Glass alone: $15-$25.

The exterior art here is extremely awkward. Her hidden arm comes down right through her belt, making it look like she has two right arms. The New York identifier is a curious touch. It's possible that like the "Miss America" travel decals, there was a nudie glass like this for every state. $15-$25.

Old and faded Meyercord Dutch girl inside and out. This may be an earlier decal than those on the sheet; the underwear inside is not much of a payoff.

Meyercord Double Face Cuties decal sheet in and out of its original packaging. All of the "types" were clearly chosen for their long and voluminous costumes. These are past being useable, but if mint, full sheet: $35-$45.

The party side of the Indian girl from the Meyercord decal sheet—all you get is a bra and panties from this gal. Extremely worn & bleached out, the decal still holds enough image to be interesting.

A morality tale in two images and 12 fluid ounces. The hitching gal with her dress hoisted up is shown inside stripped naked and catching a ride from Satan himself in his hell-bound roadster. This piece is totally unlike the others. We're seeing decal drama here, but its message is fuzzy. A warning about the perils of females hitchhiking? How both parties in the hitchhiking equation really see each other? Satan getting lucky on Route 666? Sex and sin on your glass of gin? Whatever the moral of this story is, it's great art and a rare piece indeed. (And if it was part of a set, the author would sure like to see the others.) $75.

Chapter 5

Displays

Impko window signage. Measures 5" x 4", perfect for the door of a hobby shop or bicycle shop. This one is damaged, but if primo: $20.

In the 1950s, this classic Impko sales card was hypnotic. Boys were drawn in like moths to a lamp. And at ten cents per, the decals were on equal price footing with a candy bar. Sweaty hands clutched allowance coins while little minds churned with the choices: a Three Musketeers bar or two flaming devil decals for my bicycle? Art for art's sake, or a belly full of sugar? Jujubes or flaming eyeballs on my lunchbox? These were decisions each fella had to make for himself.

This display is almost factory-fresh. Of its 50 original decals, only one is missing. The support panel in back, which allowed the display to free-stand on a counter, has not been folded out, and it was stored all these years in its original shipping bag. Measures 12.5" x 9.25".

Sold individually, the decals would bring around $250 in today's market. Value of the whole display in this pristine condition: $300-$350.

Another Impko display card, and further evidence of the near boundless scope of their offerings. The humor here is strictly *Mad* magazine. Even if Alfred E. Newman's smiling mug wasn't present, anyone who'd ever read a copy of *Mad* in the '60s would know exactly where these kinds of gags originated. Humorwise, it's not boffo material these days; dud is more like the word you're looking for.

The Beatnik Cool School decal is in an entirely separate category from the others. Everything goes in cycles, they say, and a resurgence in beatdom has been rippling through America for a few years now, bringing back coffee shops, bongos, poetry readings, and a fresh audience for the work of Kerouac and Burroughs. Maynard G. Krebs is once again the folk hero he deserves to be. The whole thing is kind of based on old media images of the beatniks, but it's sandaled heart is in the right place. Every goateed cat who's seen this display has offered a twenty to take a beatnik decal home. Neither of the two that are left have been sold, but $30 looks like an achievable price tag. None of the others would bring more than $10, and even that might be a stretch. Entire display (11" x 14") as is, with only two or three of each decal: $100.

Advertising flyer pushing free decals to retailers of New Idea farm equipment. No date, but the Ford pickup—almost certainly new at the time—is within a year either way of 1960. Flyer: $5.

Top bar from another Impko display, this one salvaged from an old bicycle shop. The rest of it is pretty well destroyed.

All-metal counter display from the alphabet side of the decal world. Measures about 11" deep, 7" wide, 13" tall, made by the Hallmark Monogram Company, Bayonne, NJ. The display is well stocked except that there's not a single letter L left. One strip of photos from the back panel is missing, but the remaining pictures suggest some very strange uses—like initials on an alligator wallet. Many decal makers strictly warned against trying to put their product on a rough leather surface, but maybe the bright boys in Bayonne knew something other people didn't. Full display, in this condition, $75-$90.

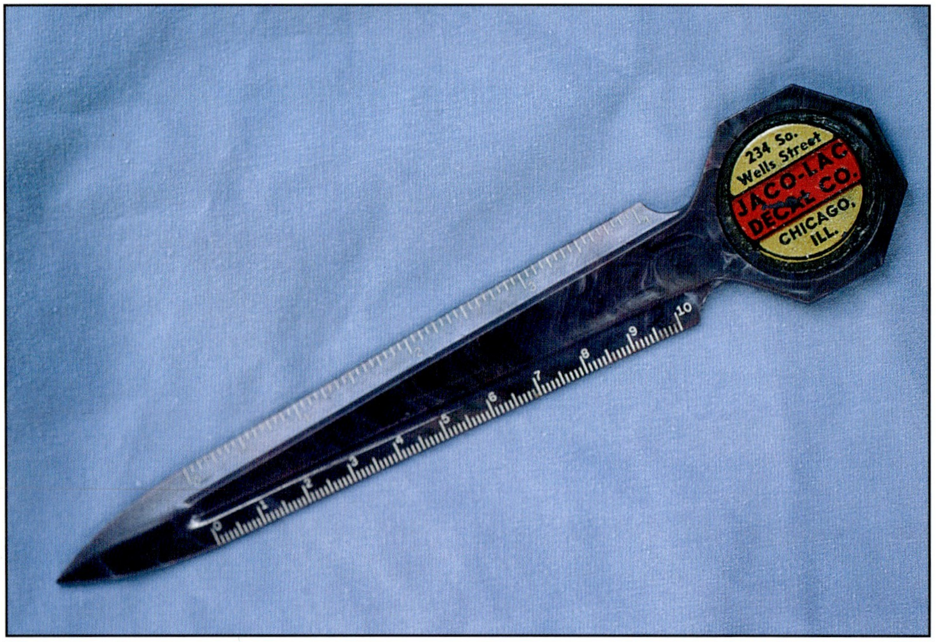

Evidently, decal makers didn't go in for promotional items. It seems as though they would have—it was a big business, and a competitive one. But if the promo lighters, pocket knives, and tape measures are out there, they're well hidden and terminally rare. Chet and Cheryl Crill, who are the crowned heads of match cover collecting, report that they've never seen a match flap from a decal company. The situation struck them as so unusual that they went into serious search mode. Six months later, still no dice. It is kind of a vexing state of non-affairs. Every filling station, corner store and sawdust tavern in America had matches made. There don't even seem to be any manufacturer/retailer splits, like "Happy's Bicycle Shop—your source for Impko decals."
The Jaco-Lac letter opener is the only such piece that's come to light. Two things are sad about the letter opener. One is that the decal is chipped. The other is that Jaco-Lac letter openers are easier to find than Jaco-Lac decals.

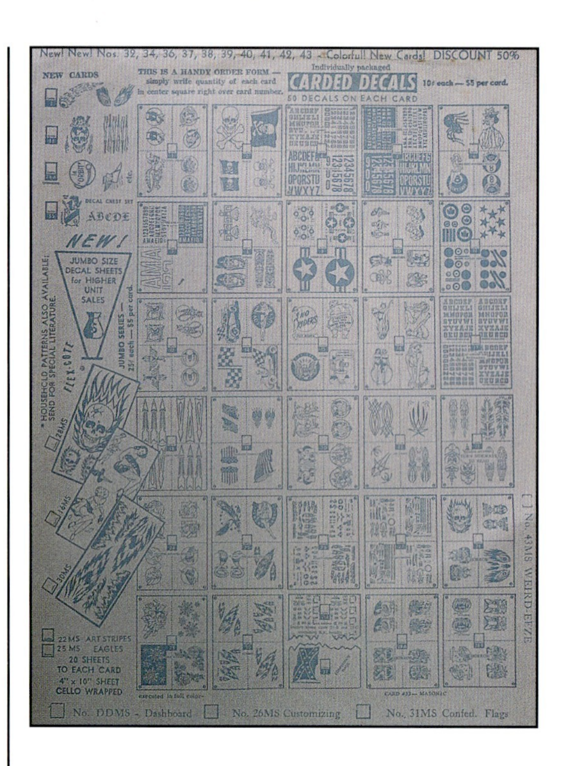

New! New! Nos. 32, 34, 36, 37, 38, 39, 40, 41, 42, 43 - Colorful! New Cards! DISCOUNT 50%

NEW CARDS

THIS IS A HANDY ORDER FORM — simply write quantity of each card in center square right over card number.

Individually packaged
CARDED DECALS 10¢ each — $5 per card.
50 DECALS ON EACH CARD

NEW!

22MS ART STRIPES
25MS EAGLES
20 SHEETS TO EACH CARD
4" x 10" SHEET
CELLO WRAPPED

No. 43MS WEIRD-EEZE

No. DDMS - Dashboard   No. 26MS Customizing   No. 31MS Confed. Flags

Impko ordering sheets, detailing the different display cards and series available.

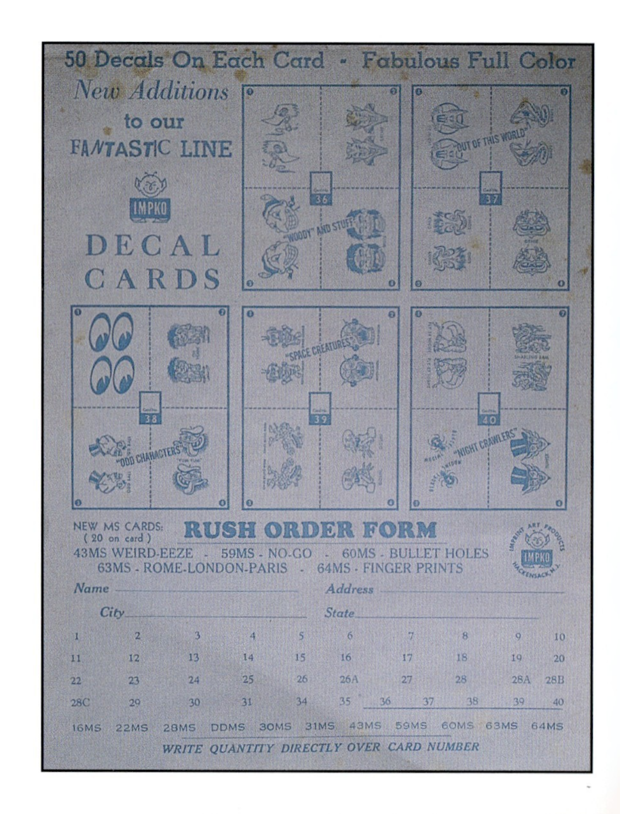

50 Decals On Each Card • Fabulous Full Color

New Additions to our FANTASTIC LINE

IMPKO

DECAL CARDS

NEW MS CARDS (20 on card)

RUSH ORDER FORM

43MS WEIRD-EEZE - 59MS - NO-GO - 60MS - BULLET HOLES
63MS - ROME-LONDON-PARIS - 64MS - FINGER PRINTS

Name ____ Address ____
City ____ State ____

1	2	3	4	5	6	7	8	9	10
11	12	13	14	15	16	17	18	19	20
22	23	24	25	26	26A	27	28	28A	28B
28C	29	30	31	34	35	36	37	38	39	40
16MS	22MS	28MS	DDMS	30MS	31MS	43MS	59MS	60MS	63MS	64MS

WRITE QUANTITY DIRECTLY OVER CARD NUMBER

Chapter 6

ART LAC Magazine

It was 1946—the war had just ended. As a major naval port, sunny San Diego had been a hub of frantic activity since the Japanese bombed Pearl Harbor late in 1941. From a print shop on Fifth Avenue, Arthur Braunstein opened an interesting little chapter in decal history.

Art Lac: The Decal Magazine combined photos and short stories with actual color decals that readers could cut out and use. The full-page decal sheets were bound in with the paper, and the only way to tell the decals from the regular pages was that the decals were shiny. The Winter, 1946 issue of *Art Lac* had seven pages of decals out of 32 pages total—other issues had a different page count and decal ratio. It was a digest-sized publication, measuring 8.25" x 5.25", with a cover price of 25 cents. A yearly subscription (four issues) cost $1.00.

Winter, 1946 was their third issue. The content was mainly swimsuit promotional photos of actresses—Ann Sheridan (Warner Bros.), Claire Trevor (RKO), and Acquanetta (Monogram) were among those who had their pictures featured on plain paper without any stories. Martha Vickers, Jean Stevans, and Beryl Wallace were immortalized as full-page *Art Lac* decals. A photo of actor Van Johnson and a black-bordered memorial portrait of the late Franklin D. Roosevelt were also decals. In addition, there were two pages of cartoon art—one for kids (Kiddecals), and the other, with silhouetted nudes and a leering wolf (Daddecals), targeted at men. The copy in *Art Lac* was limited to short essays extolling the great past and promising future of decals, the many uses decals could be put to, and their importance in the modern world—plus all the ways that the publishers of *Art Lac* could tailor custom decals to your every need.

Art Lac was doomed to a short life: it was a novelty, and its content was so strange that it's hard to guess who its audience might have been. Besides, it was an expensive novelty—a copy of *Life* magazine was only 10 cents in 1946.

A related effort appeared in 1987. Serge Clerc, a well-known French comic artist and illustrator, brought out a booklet with four pages of waterslide transfers called *Decalo*, featuring girls done in his distinctive style.

Art Lac number 3, Winter 1946

Beryl Wallace, an Earl Carroll star, as a full page *Art Lac* decal.

Full-page Jean Stevans decal, with a couple fishie fans added. Why one fishie has wings and the other a top hat remains a mystery.

The late President Roosevelt takes his place in decal history.

"Daddecals" for men. It's not overly attractive art. The 25 cents it cost to pick up a copy of *Art Lac* would buy a fella some red-hot pin-up decals elsewhere.

French comic artist Serge Clerc brought out the *Decalo* booklet in 1987—a truly ballsy choice of format for his artwork.

Page from *Decalo*.

Chapter 7

Transplants

From the 1930s through the 1950s, the skirt-chasing wolf was a seminal image. He starred in Tex Avery cartoons and appeared on cocktail napkins and nudie playing cards. *Rogue* magazine adopted the wolf as a mascot. In early issues it was a literal portrayal; later they stylized it. As a predator on the make, the wolf was always decked out in a tux or a zoot suit. Tex Avery put his wolves behind the wheel of long, sleek two-seater convertibles—the better to scoop up dates with, grandma.

The decal wolf is a well-traveled image. It has been tattooed on people countless times, and famous Honolulu tattooer Sailor Jerry Collins used this exact wolf on a flash sheet. The Wolf Patrol license plate is a rare 1950s car accessory. A car aerial pennant with similar art was sold at the same time.

The Impko wolf decals are about 2" in diameter. $10 the pair. Cheap for an image with so much history.

This piece didn't translate very well. The "Miss America" decal art is beautiful. On the drinking glass she's not only gotten ugly and hard around the face, but one breast is now significantly larger than the other and her leg is curved like a snake with a shoe on the end. Decal, if mint, $15.

Decal art has often served as inspiration for tattooing, but this is an extremely unusual choice. It works well, though. Tattoo is on Paul Bearer's hand. Octopus decals by Impko, $10 the pair.

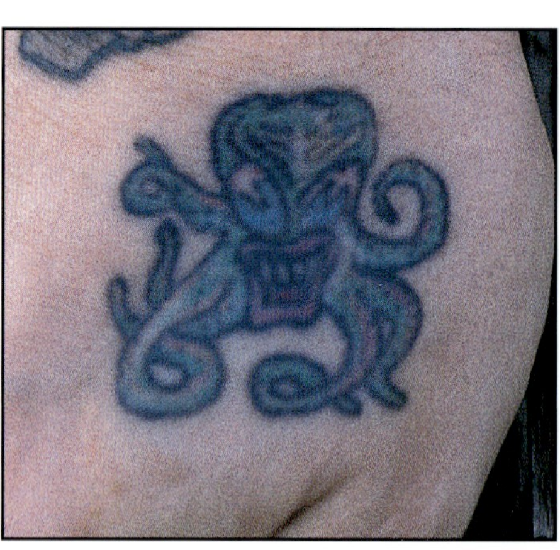

Chapter 8

Hot Rods & Cool Designs

Custom cars and hot rods today are part of a sharply divided subculture. On the one hand, you have modern street rods. They are expensive, fiberglass-bodied toys, loaded down with air conditioning and digital amenities, fitted with cushy modern suspensions, shiny with trend-of-the-moment paint schemes. Aside from the body style, they have no more to do with the past than a fresh Big Mac—and they have a Big Mac level of soul. Fans of these cars trailer them around to shows and family-style gatherings, whoop it up under the speed limit for a day or two, and trailer them safely home. The whole scene is a Happy Days/American Grafitti fabrication, with Betty Boop dragged in for good measure. One of the biggest family-style modern-rodding organizations is called the Good Guys.

But hot rods were originated by Bad Guys. That was the point. Hot rods and customs in the 50s and 60s were home-built war wagons of rebellion and anarchy, and rodding richly deserved its evil reputation in the 1950s and 60s.

This is the other side of the fence today, where those vintage war wagons still live—steel-bodied, loud, leaky, about half safe—same as they were 40-plus years ago. Unlike the modern copies, most of these bombs are owner-built, using period-correct parts, with no updated concepts involved.

Vintage rod & custom decals offer an unfiltered link to those greasy old days. As more and more people turn away from the ersatz American Grafitti thing and start nosing around for the real stuff, the decals gain in popularity. If online auctions are a reliable indicator, their popularity has literally erupted over the past couple years.

And with good reason. Speed equipment and other custom decals offer graphics that are unavailable anywhere else. Many of the old rodding images would have been lost except for the surviving decals.

It's also worth mentioning—and this is kind of a downbeat facet—that car decals may be the first place where American consumers showed their willingness to pay for the privilege of advertising someone else's product. Between Old Navy and Nike and Abercrombie and Fitch *ad nauseum*, the concept that "I will pay to carry your name around town" is so much a part of today's consumer landscape that it's hard to imagine a time when it didn't exist. But there was such a time. And tracing back through old car magazines, one can see that by 1960, some companies had stopped advertising their products altogether and gone for the decal dollar instead. That may be the exact point where the landscape shifted.

It's a weird image and a weirder motto, seeing as Traction Masters didn't sell cooling parts. $10-$15.

From Impko, with a friendly wave to all. Near Mint: $15-$20.

Launched in the late 1940s, Iskenderian has been one of the most successful and visible racing cam companies ever since. In 1961, a full-page ad read: "Iskenderian set a new standard for 'perfection' by employing the use of the famous IBM Computor [sic]... the instrument by which the far-advanced Iskenderian Polydyne Proflles were evolved. Virtually every Isky grind now features the Polydyne Profile, recognized as the optimum solution to efficient cam design." There couldn't have been more than half a dozen computers in the world in 1961, and here's a hotrodder plotting cam angles with one. Along with forward-looking engineering, Isky did a lot of decal advertising. Polydyne decal is about 8" across and 6" tall—large by automotive decal standards. $15.

A real classic, and one that stayed popular well into the 1960s. The word on the bottom was changed innumerable times, to read everything from "Money," to "Pontiac," "Ford," and all the other car brand names. Dealers carried a whole spin-rack of variations of this decal. "Powered by Junk" was always a top seller. Most variations are not hard to find today. Made by Ed Cholakian Enterprises. $5-$10.

An Impko gag decal. No idea why the doggy is there. $8.

Gag racing decal—made after 1964. $10-$15.

Another gag racing decal, with much more pointed humor. This was a direct burn on the "Dedicated to Safety" NHRA decal, which had official variations for both race participants and winners. As for New York City's Connecting Highway, the Apple was going through a tremendous urban renewal building period in the 1960s, and this had to be a stretch of temporarily unnamed freeway taken over in the wee hours for speed contests. The squad car chasing the rail is a great graphic. $15-$20.

The enraptured, stockinged gal riding the long, hard Custom Cam was an instant success. It's being reproduced today as a sticker, and it's still a success. Originally available as both a right and left facing image, the left-facing decal is much harder to find. Right: $15. Left: $25. Pair: $40.

One of the most memorable images in all of speed equipment history. Hillborn was a pioneer in fuel injection technology and this decal drove it home in a way no one could forget. $20-$25.

The STP sticker was possibly the most recognizable graphic in America through the 1960s. They were everywhere. It was reported in 1968 that STP owner Andy Granatelli gave away 2 million of the red, white and blue ovals every month. Twenty-four million stickers a year is a lot of publicity. This LSD decal—a rare piece of psychedelic humor—apes Granatelli's sticker perfectly, except for the letters. $10-$15.

Hurst was *the* name in shifters, and they issued dozens of decal designs. The 6" ball is one of the tougher ones to find. $15-$20.

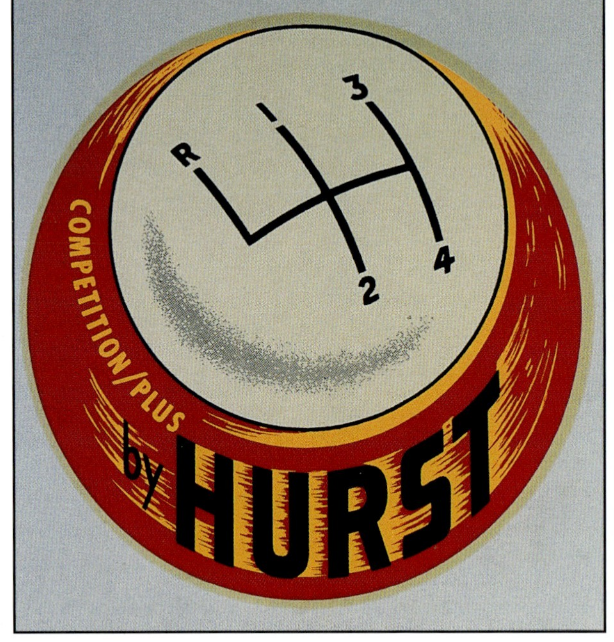

Offenhauser built race cars and racing parts that had style and class. Many of their speed parts were things of true beauty. Unfortunately, they put out one ugly decal. $10.

Direct, classy, and to the point exactly. $10.

NHRA-sanctioned drag race decal from the Northern New Jersey area. Independent strips frequently designed their own decals, often with great graphics. This one's a peach. Value depends on local interest and history. $15.

Steen made go-kart racing parts and chemicals, and were one of the biggest names in karting, which was itself a big business hrough the 1960s. 5" tall. $10.

Another outstanding drag decal, but from a much higher-profile race, which brings its value up. $30.

Waterslide decal from an even higher profile Indianapolis motoring event. Today's stickers are identical. $15.

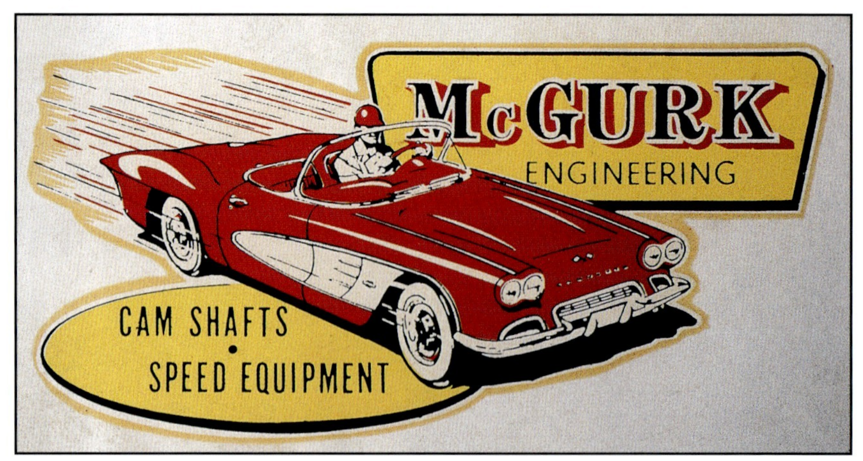

McGurk was a major name in speed parts, and they had a fantastic decal, too. Very difficult to find. $25-$30.

For those who like to advertise their reading tastes. 4" across. $5-$10.

Decals from some local speed and performance businesses bring a good price—as with drag decals, it depends on the location and the history. The Valley Head Service decal was a crowd pleaser around LA—the San Fernando Valley being the geographical depression in question. Frequently the V in Valley would be blotted out or covered in black, leaving simply "alley Head Service," which was considered absolutely hilarious in garages and auto parts stores. Tough to find. $25.

Decal ads from 1961. Sturtevant had decided to soft-pedal parts in favor of decals, and the other company offered a way for enthusiasts to score in bulk.

--DECALS--

Original Speed Mfg. Decals

Engle Cams	C & T Automotive
Moon Equip.	Edelbrock Equip.
Schiefer	Eelco Mfg. (foot prints)
Weiand Equip.	Weber Cams
Howard's Cams	Offenhauser Equip.
Clay Smith Cams	Crankshaft Co.
Reath Auto	Speed Spec.
Isky Cams	Grant Piston Rings
Jahn's Pistons	Mickey Thompson Enterprises

Your choice 5 for $1.00
Our choice 10 for $1.00
Extra Large Decals $1.00 each
Complete selection $3.00

Act Now for Complete Selection
(No C.O.D — Prepaid Only) Write to:

DE-CAL ENTERPRISES
Box 806, Pacific Palisades, Calif.

DECEMBER, 1961

Honest Charley was sort of a small-scale, southern, J.C. Whitney offering parts of all kinds by mail. The chicken with the cigarette holder bears some small family resemblance to the famous cigar-chomping Clay Smith Cams woodpecker. There are right and left versions of this, and later versions with the chicken in a muscle car. Hard decal to find: $25.

An ethnic slur, hot rod style. Like the slick-and-mag decal with "Powered by Junk" (or anything else), there were "Genuine Parts" decals for all the same things—junk parts, Buick parts, Ford parts—and another classic, "Genuine Stolen Parts." This south-of-the-border entry had nothing to do with Chicano pride—it was a slur that meant junk parts. $10.

Pair of decals for Foxcraft accessories—the fender skirts girl has a lot of charm, and fender skirts themselves are not something you see advertised much. Neither is useable, but even in this shape, $15 each.

Original famous Moon waterslide decal, still a hugely popular image: $10.

Always popular, always in good taste, equally useful for truckers or car owners. No maker's name on this one. $10.

Although not strictly a car decal, Hot Head is a timeless design, and the flaming, bullet-holed skull was extremely popular around anything mechanical. The large one is just under 4" tall, the smaller ones, 2" tall. Large: $10-$15. Small: $10 the pair.

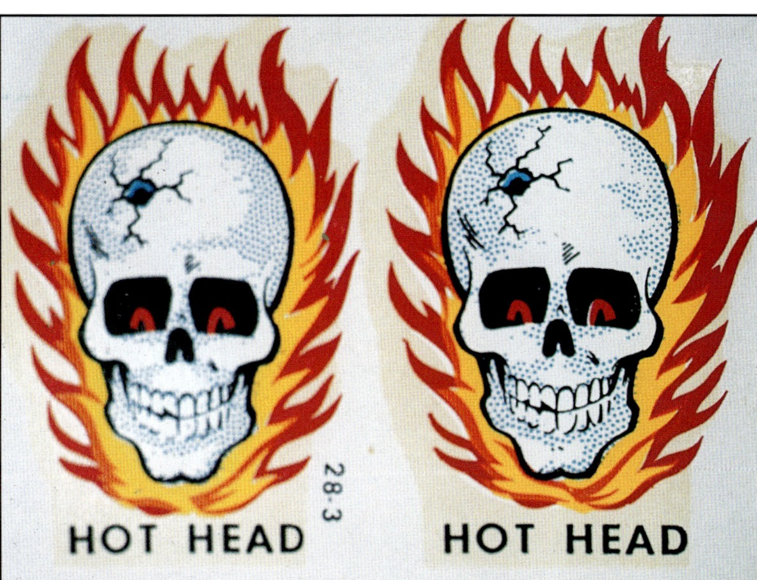

Impko dame with a delicate rear—good for a laugh in almost any parking lot. Scarce. $20.

Impko girl and her race car—note her understated crash helmet. Kind of an odd image to want on your car. $10-$15

There's no rational explanation, but Impko marketed these 10" tall sheets of fingerprint decals to an automotive clientele. If it was a fad, it was small and over quickly. Sheet: $5.

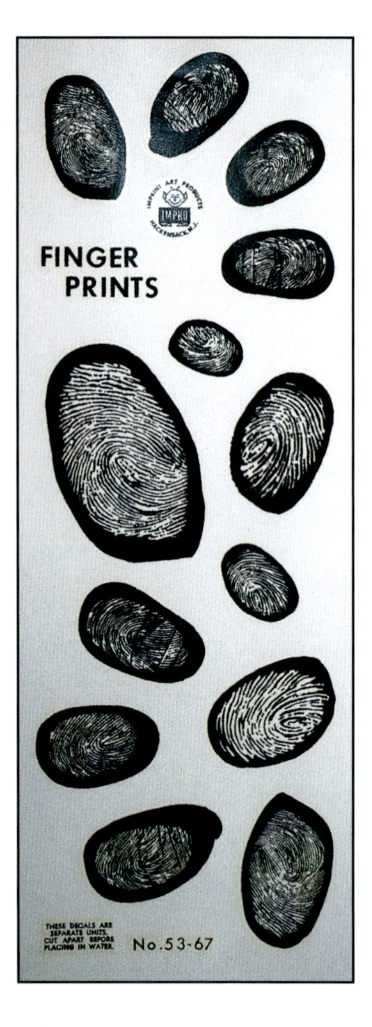

Vintage waterslide NASCAR decal. 5" long. $10.

This one's just hilarious. A guy in horse-jockey racing silks riding a flathead piston: Why? A girl in a bikini would have made this a truly great decal—as it is, it's just about as silly as art gets. $2 if you're lucky.

A classic, this one from Impko, 4" long. $5

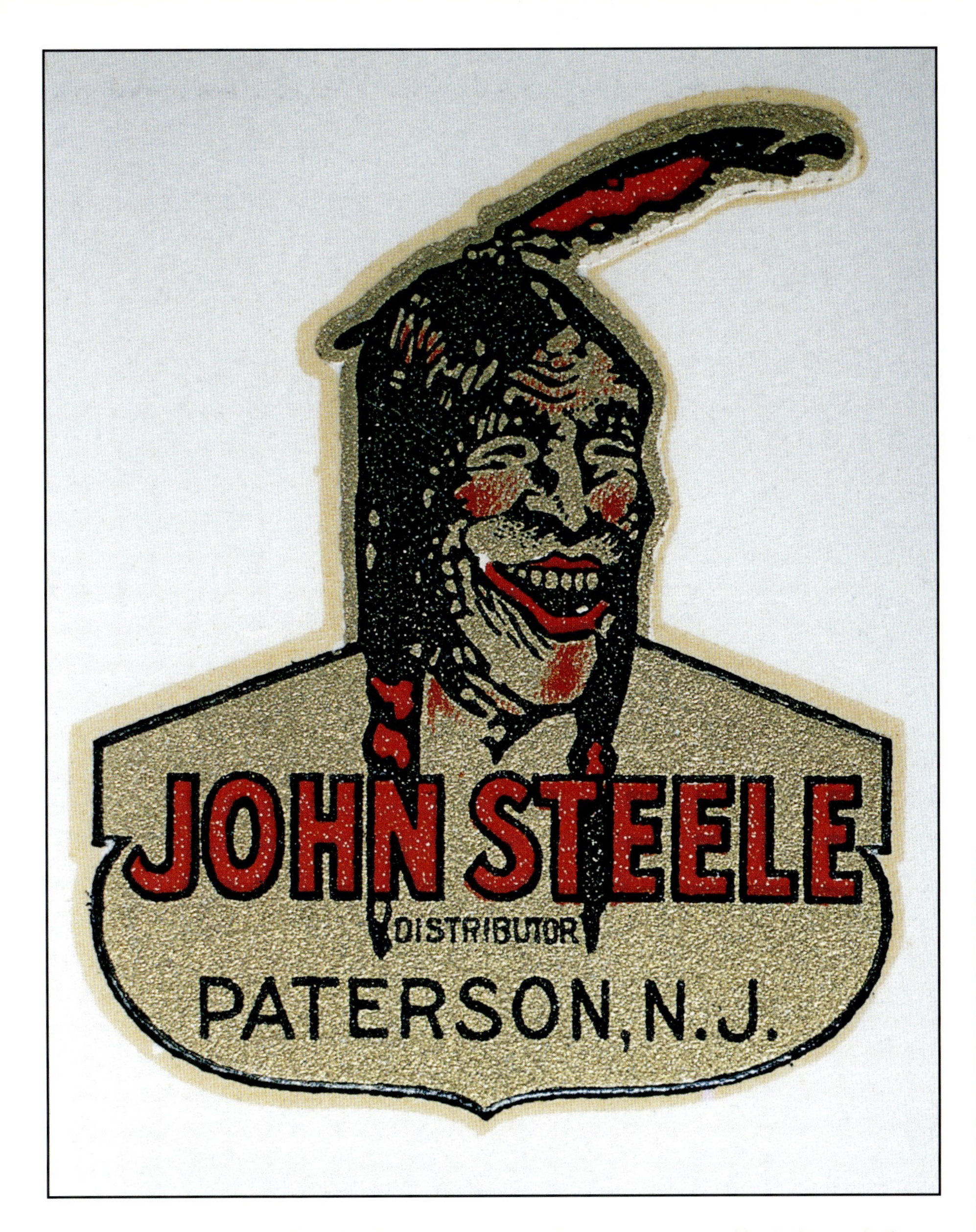

Extremely rare to find old dealership decals, especially from a marque like Indian, which went out of business in 1953. The laughing Indian, as the stories go, was a patch that early Wigwam racers had sewn onto the seat of their pants; as they passed the competition, they'd raise up off the seat and give 'em the business. This is a tiny decal, just 1.5" tall, but will easily bring $25.

Great name for a bike club, and a businesslike logo. $15.

Factory original Cushman Eagle tank decal. This one has been in the author's collection for more than 30 years. $35-$40.

These are class all the way. Through the annals of motoring, a lot of thought and poetry has gone into trying to keep idiots from passing on the right when trucks are involved. Big rig staples include:

Overtaker	Undertaker
Safe Side	Suicide
Traffic Beater	Meet St. Peter

This gorgeous Impko pair is the decal version, although a little small for a big truck. Complete sheet: 10" tall. $30.

Not specifically for cars, but a great addition to cool wheels nonetheless, the tumbling dice showing lucky seven was always a winner. $10.

Although fairly small, the right and left flaming eyes must have been intended for either cars or bicycles with tanks. $10.

It would be semi-clever if the truck were actually a pickup. Impko. $10.

Impko's version of the Jolly Roger—good for cars, motorcycles, go-karts, or anywhere else a fella wanted that bad-attitude look. Jolly Roger probably has a significantly different twist in meaning if you're English—and the majority of classical pirates were. Rogering, in the Queen's slang, is the equivalent of screwing—so giving a ship the Jolly Roger was pretty raw. $10 will get these bones today.

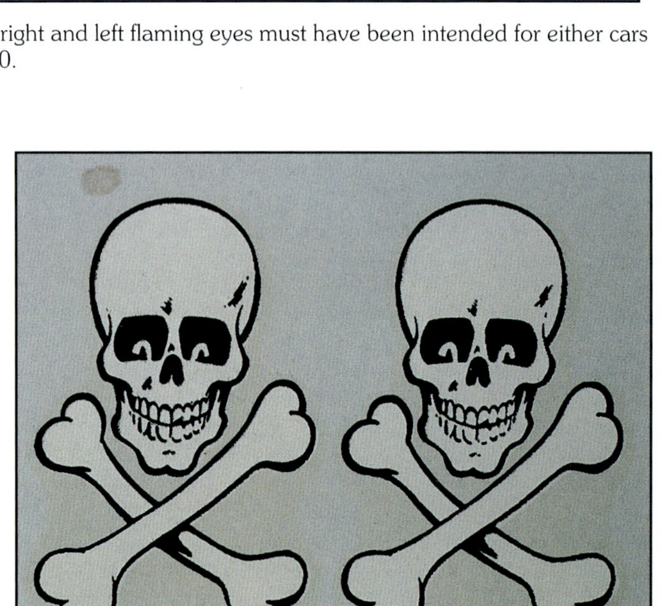

Great art and eye-catching design on this piece. Impko. $12-18.

Chapter 9

Monsters & Aliens

The 1950s were especially fruitful years for monsters, aliens and robots. Movies brought aliens to Earth and put Earthmen into space; celluloid monsters came from swamps, the sea, the sewers; robots clanked after human prey, and someone saved Hitler's brain. The Blob chased Steve McQueen all over town in the relentless quest for teenage blood. The night had a thousand eyes and there was a beast with five fingers.

The real-life atom bomb was here to stay, and people sweated the adjustment to that fact. For the first time, we could truly destroy the planet—or more likely, the Russians would. The atom bomb also introduced a thing called radiation. The movies ran with the ball: radiation mutated good men into bad monsters, or left their faces a melted wreck. It spawned giant ants, towering spiders, behemoth lizards. Everything cinematic radiation touched came after humans for either food or vengeance.

And filmic scientists were worse than juvenile delinquents. Who knew what vile, jar-born horror might issue from some mad scientist's lab, followed by an echoing, evil laugh?

The kids who dug the fright flicks couldn't get enough, and the decalcomaniacs at Impko, especially, came through for them with what they called their "Fantastic Line." Among Impko's monster offerings were a series of great images made just the right size for a horror-obsessed boy to put on his bicycle—which thousands of boys did. Other companies swung with their own monsters as best they could.

A strange size (3.5" across) but otherwise absolutely typical of an Impko monster face—just plain weird, and very colorful. $10.

These look like perverted beatnik Scrubbing Bubbles, complete with the classic hot rod monster lolling tongue. Impko. $5-$10.

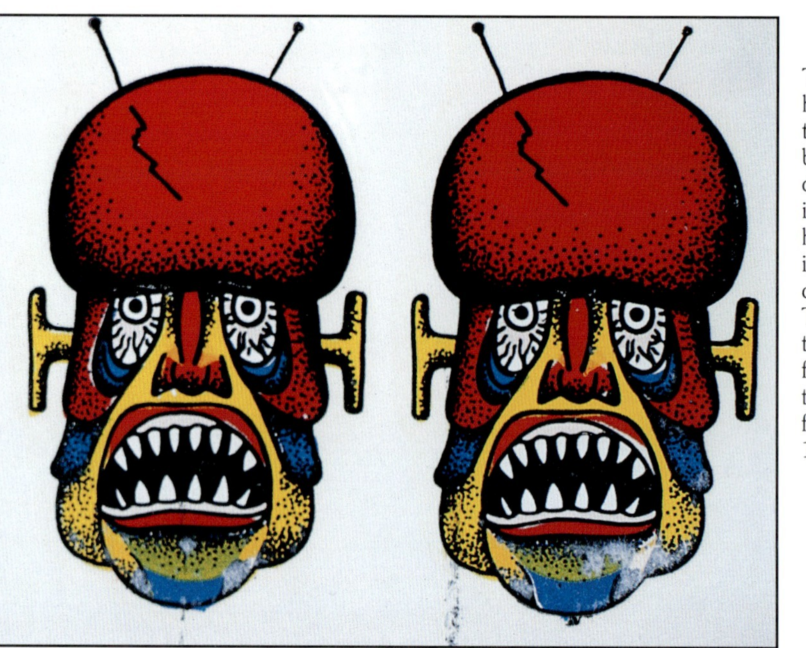

The antennae and T-handle ears tell you they're aliens; the bloodshot eyes and distressed expression indicates maybe they had a little too much intergalactic truck-stop coffee on the way here. They look more pained than menacing. Impko faces in the classic two-to-a-sheet size: each face approx. 2" tall and 1.5" wide. $5-$10.

The unrestrained use of color elevates these otherwise pedestrian faces to the level of truly magnificent art. The beatnik influence of the 1950s is obvious. Impko. $10 and well worth it.

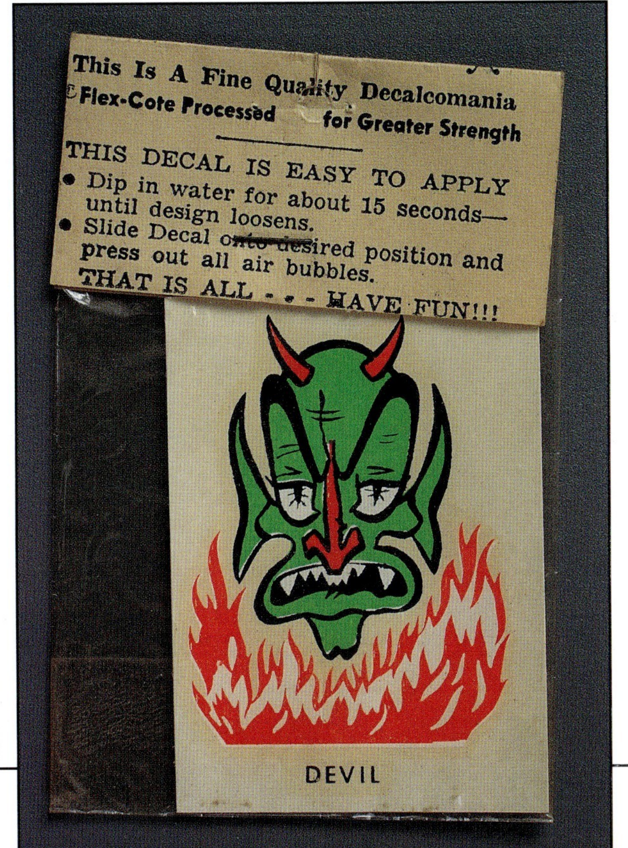

One of Impko's all-time finest designs, shown two different color/ways. The solo package of the green devil is unusual—it is evidently factory Impko work, since the copy mentions their Flex-Cote process—but this fella, like the rest, was usually sold as a sheet of two. $10.

Melting pitchfork lizard terror from beyond the stars. Impko. $5-$10.

The ambulatory chancre seeks access to the top of the power structure. It's what all aliens wanted in the 1950s; nowdays they want to blend in and hide. Impko. $10.

Terrific robots of the tin-can school. Name-wise, it seems maybe the Impko artists had a hat full of words that might vaguely relate to monsters and science fiction, and pulled out two random nouns. Nothing could be less appropriate than calling these guys zombies, and sonar just adds to the confusion. $10.

There was a kind of fascination with headsmen and beheading in the 50s that went along with the whole horror thing. These swingin' axe men were Impko's contribution. $5-$10.

Ever so evil, but very well dressed. Impko. $5-$10.

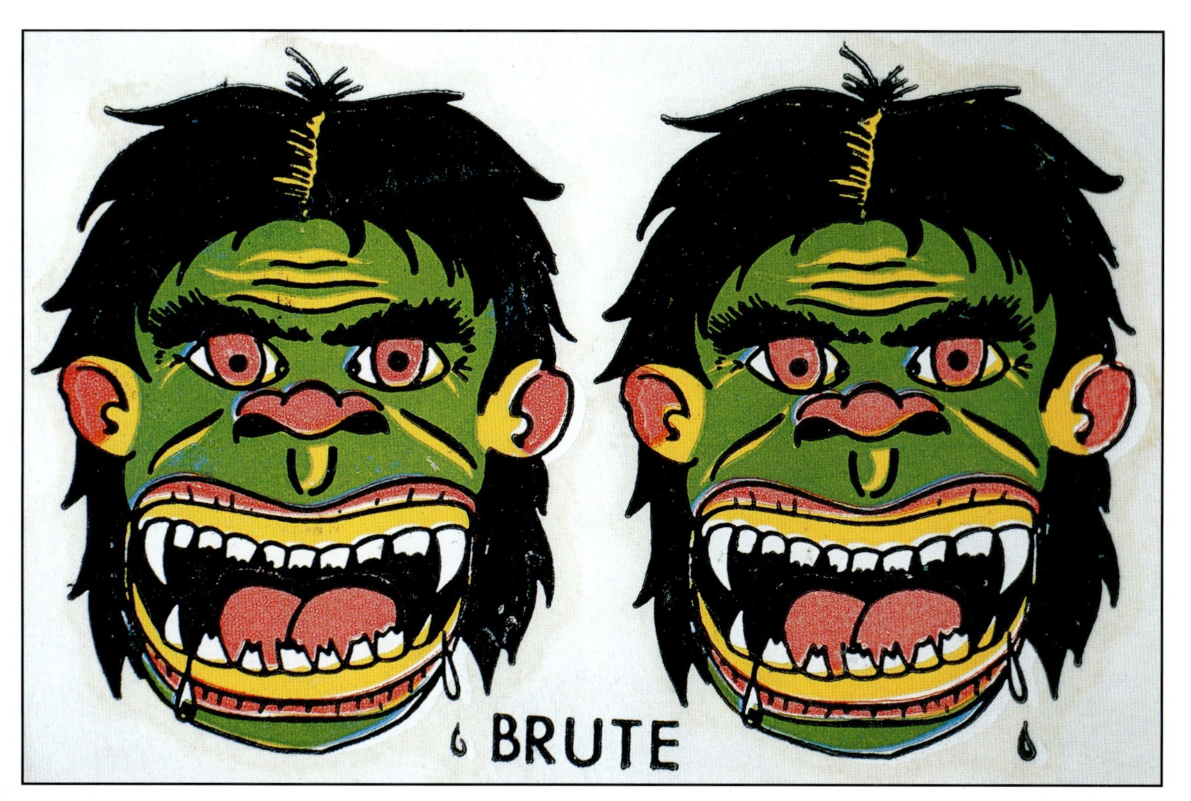

When looking for menace, let's not forget our simian population. Impko. $5-$10.

The Shape ... it comes in the night seeking acne medication. Impko. $5-$10.

This is totally killer art. With the flames and Abba-Zaba checkered trousers on the dapper devil, it's as fresh and relevant today as it was forty-some years ago—maybe more so. Not surprisingly, it has been copied in recent years and sold as a sticker. Difficult to find. Impko. $10-$20.

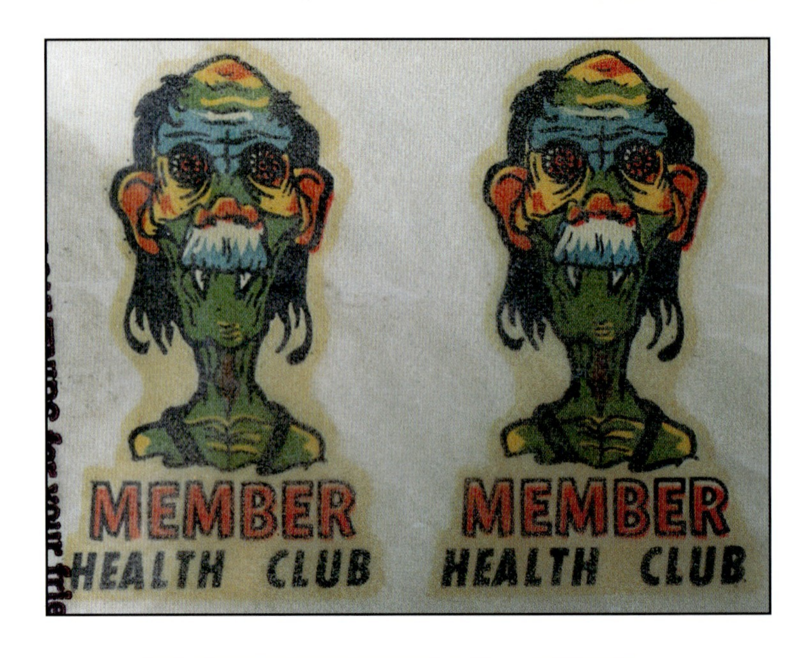

Another of Impko's more enduring images, shown in two color/ways. The greenish version is the more common of the two; sadly, that sheet is permanently stuck inside its glassine bag. $5-$10.

A pompadoured guy with amphetamine eyes and a stubby, muscular arm ending in a lumpy boxing glove, trailing hot rod scallops, and rendered entirely in earth tones—you have to wonder what they were thinking. It measures 5.5" long and just over 1" at its tallest spot—perfect dimensions for the top tube of a bicycle frame, which is almost certainly where it was meant to go. Still, what kind of message are we getting here? Punch 'Em All, Let God Sort 'Em Out? Jab first, ask questions later? No maker's name. $5-$10.

There's a strong Buck Rogerish feel to this enigmatic decal. No maker's mark. It could easily have come from a cereal box, or a toy, or as a promotion from one of the non-network children's TV shows that filled the after-school airwaves back then—it's not hard to imagine a Space Kaydet Klub membership card. $10.

If they had given this guy a red face and hands and made him into a regular devil, it would have made sense. As it is, he looks like a lightning-borne refugee from a Halloween party. No maker's mark and no class. 3" diameter. $2.

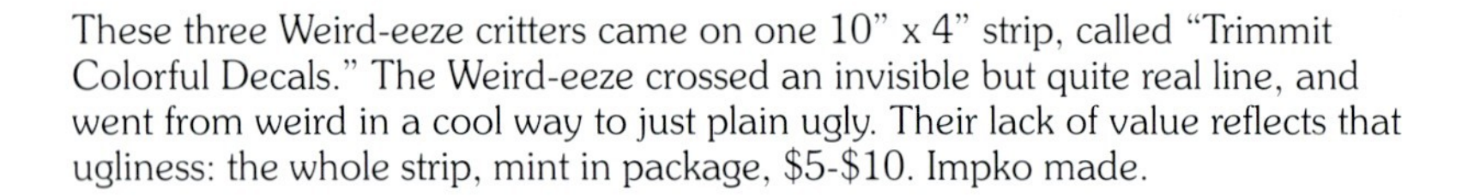

These three Weird-eeze critters came on one 10" x 4" strip, called "Trimmit Colorful Decals." The Weird-eeze crossed an invisible but quite real line, and went from weird in a cool way to just plain ugly. Their lack of value reflects that ugliness: the whole strip, mint in package, $5-$10. Impko made.

The motorcyclist is the only Hip-*eeze* variation of the Weird-*eeze* that's come to light, but it's enough. Art this bad can't be saved just by changing the name and color/way. $5 if you're lucky.

Davey is a Weird-Oh—as opposed to a Weird-eeze—which is a very important distinction. Weird-Ohs started life in the early 1960s as plastic kits from Hawk Model Company in Chicago. The Weird-Ohs series—including Digger, Davey, Daddy, the Drag Hag, Endsville Eddy and Huey Hut Rod—were pretty successful. The art was solid throughout the series and the models looked good when built. The 4" x 6" decals, also made by Hawk, are harder to find than the models. Davey, the only Weird-Oh on a bike, is by far the least valuable of the series decals. Even so, in near-mint condition Davey will bring $15-$25. The other Weird-Ohs range around $25-$35 each.

The famous Freddie Flypogger, brainchild of Stanley Mouse. Based in Detroit instead of on the West Coast, Mouse Studios' great designs gave Big Daddy Roth some serious monster competition during the early 1960s. By 1967, Mouse had disengaged from monsters altogether and was producing brilliant psychedelic poster art for concerts in San Francisco. He's had a tremendously successful career in rock'n'roll art, and is still at work in Northern California. This Freddie Flypogger decal is a large 8" x 10" and like all vintage Mouse hot rod items, it's very tough to find. *Used with permission.* $50-$75.

Chapter 10

Original Decals by Monté

There was only one bicycle shop within pedaling distance of my house in 1959: Jones and Sons.

The shop sold new and used bicycles, parts and accessories, and was a factory authorized Schwinn dealership. They only carried one line of decals: Original Decals by Monté. Throughout my important formative years, this was what a decal meant to me: Monté's very odd monsters with strange captions.

Monté was extremely talented. I have been unable to come up with any information about him at all, despite a great deal of research. He was evidently a localized southern California phenomenon, and a small time player even in that hungry market. His decals today are unbelievably rare. It was probably 1965 when I last poked a nose into Jones' shop, right about when they closed for good. In the 37 or so years since—37 years of active digging through junk, vintage, and second-hand goods across America and overseas—I've seen exactly one Monté decal for sale. It wasn't one of his best, and it was priced too high, so I let it go.

What you see here is even rarer than his decals—five complete full-color salesman's sample pages. Finding these was a Holy Grail score, because they show the range of his art so fully. There's only one design I recall that's not shown—a pinstripe pattern with "go to hell" cleverly twined into it.

Monté's art is highly idiosyncratic. He worked common themes of the day, aliens, loose eyeballs, beheading, skulls, daggers, monsters; but he did it in his own style and his own way. He added captions that were sometimes bizarre in their inappropriateness, and heavy on the rock'n'roll references.

There are a number of similarities between Monté's art and Impko's, so either somebody was copying or Monté sold designs to Impko. For sure it wasn't the other way around. The decals as shown on the salesman's pages were close to actual size—about 2" tall. His stuff was all very small, a lot of detailing packed into a tiny space. The monsters and skulls translated into that small format okay, but the pinstripe designs and flames looked like refugees from a model car kit.

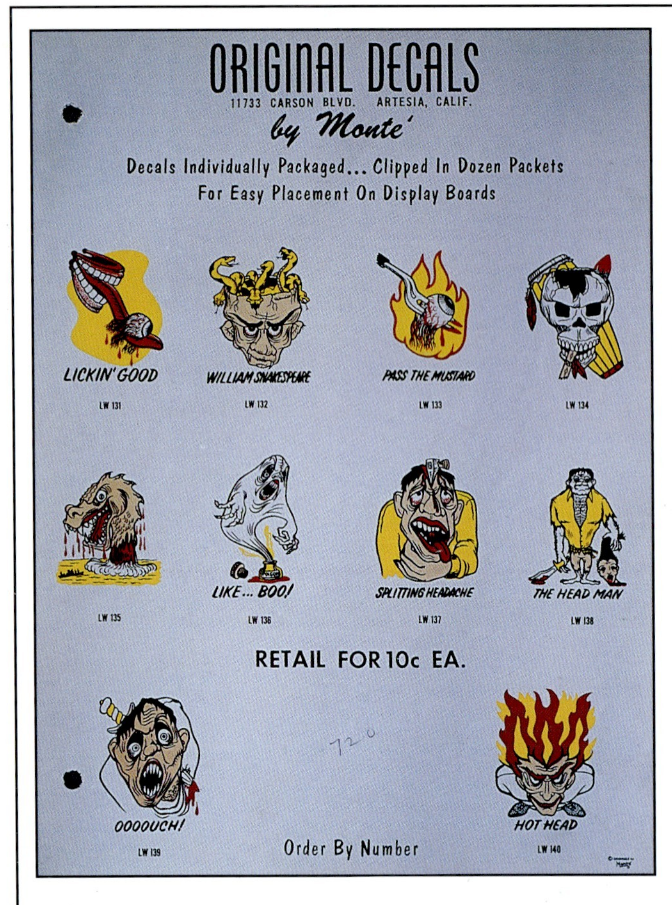
ORIGINAL DECALS
11733 CARSON BLVD. ARTESIA, CALIF.
by Monte'
Decals Individually Packaged... Clipped In Dozen Packets
For Easy Placement On Display Boards
LICKIN' GOOD
LW 131
WILLIAM SHAKESPEARE
LW 132
PASS THE MUSTARD
LW 133
LW 134
LW 135
LIKE... BOO!
LW 136
SPLITTING HEADACHE
LW 137
THE HEAD MAN
LW 138
RETAIL FOR 10c EA.
OOOOUCH!
LW 139
720
HOT HEAD
LW 140
Order By Number

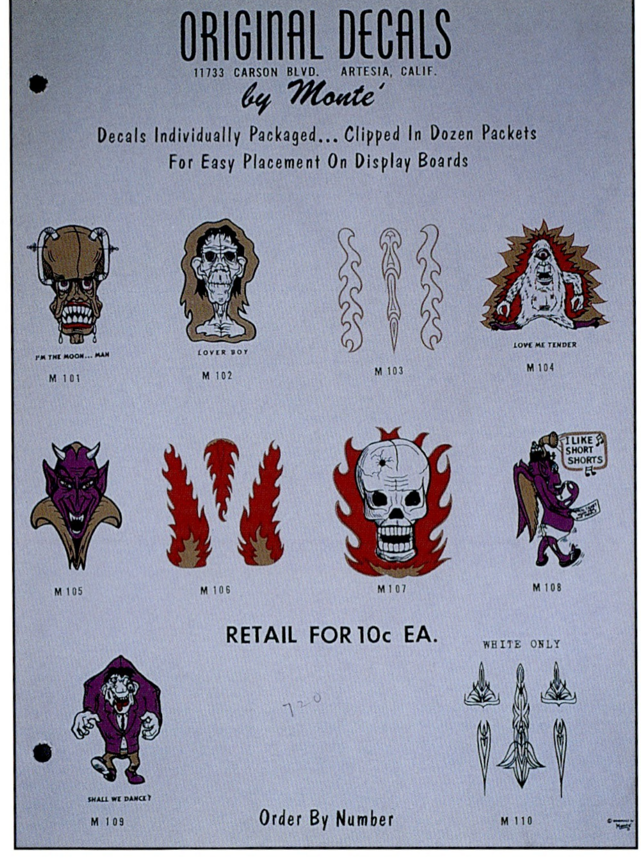
ORIGINAL DECALS
11733 CARSON BLVD. ARTESIA, CALIF.
by Monte'
Decals Individually Packaged... Clipped In Dozen Packets
For Easy Placement On Display Boards
I'M THE MOON... MAN
M 101
LOVER BOY
M 102
M 103
LOVE ME TENDER
M 104
I LIKE SHORT SHORTS
M 105
M 106
M 107
M 108
RETAIL FOR 10c EA.
WHITE ONLY
720
SHALL WE DANCE?
M 109
Order By Number
M 110

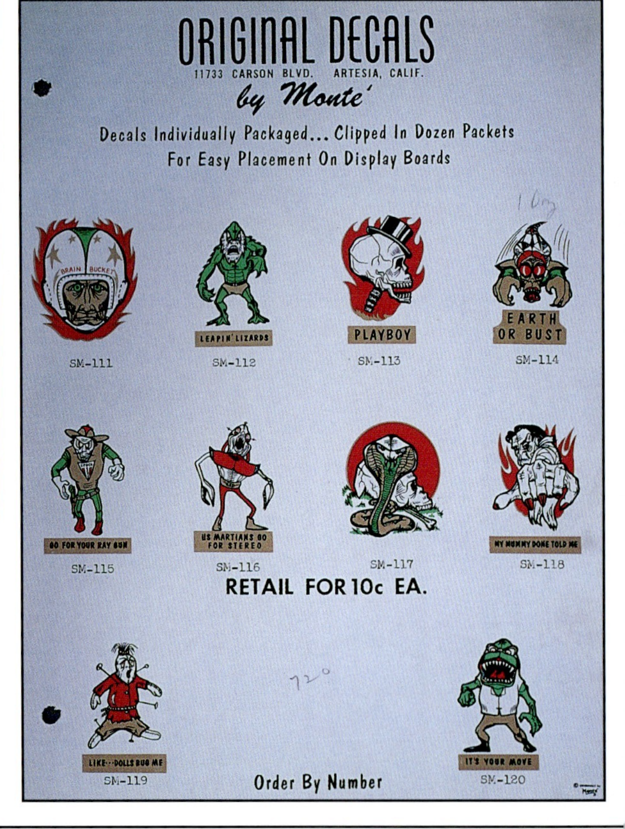
ORIGINAL DECALS
11733 CARSON BLVD. ARTESIA, CALIF.
by Monte'
Decals Individually Packaged... Clipped In Dozen Packets
For Easy Placement On Display Boards
BRAIN BUCKET
SM-111
LEAPIN' LIZARDS
SM-112
PLAYBOY
SM-113
EARTH OR BUST
SM-114
GO FOR YOUR RAY GUN
SM-115
US MARTIANS GO FOR STEREO
SM-116
SM-117
MY MOMMY DONE TOLD ME
SM-118
RETAIL FOR 10c EA.
720
LIKE--DOLLS BUG ME
SM-119
IT'S YOUR MOVE
SM-120
Order By Number

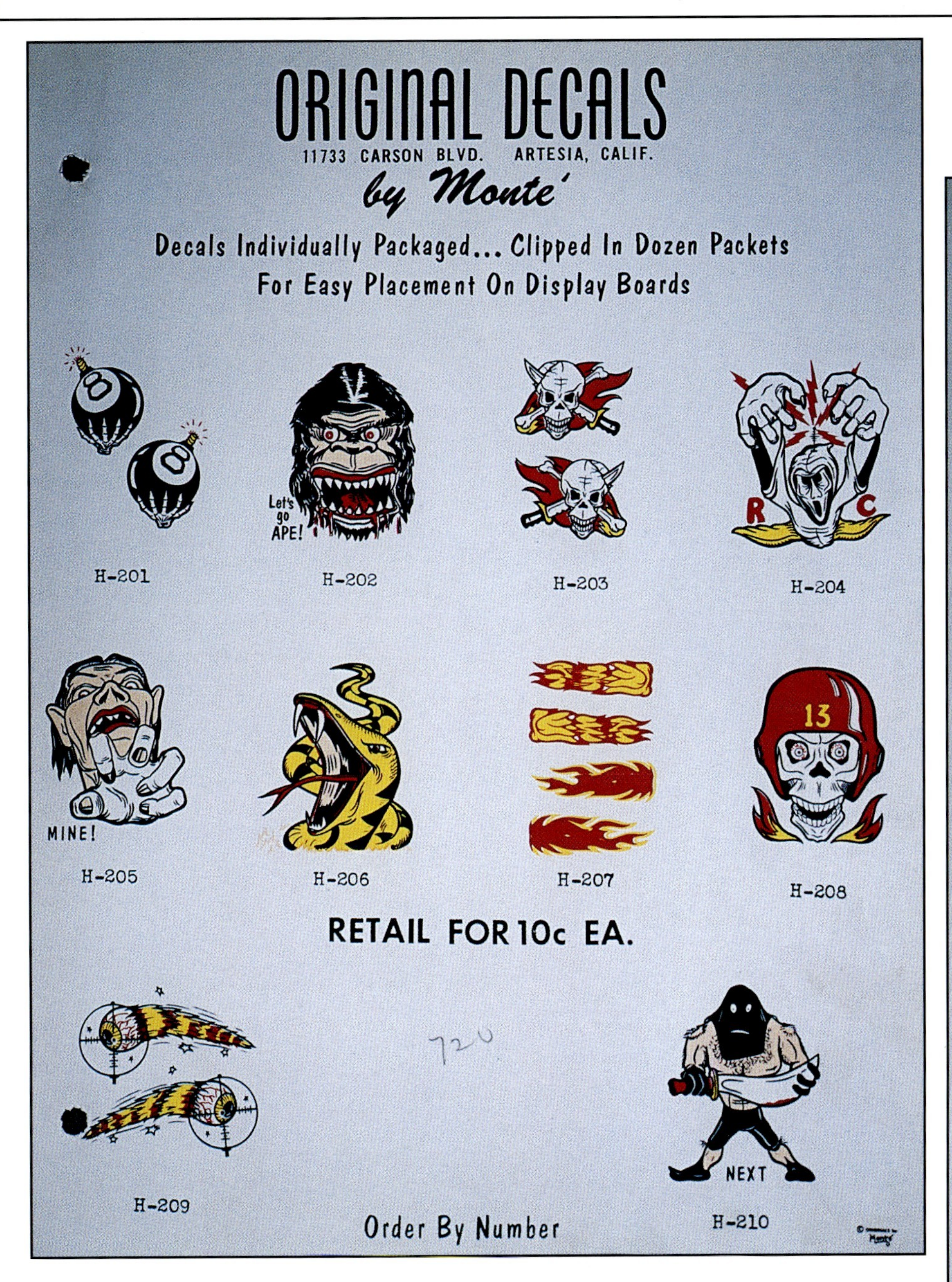
ORIGINAL DECALS
11733 CARSON BLVD. ARTESIA, CALIF.
by Monte'
Decals Individually Packaged... Clipped In Dozen Packets
For Easy Placement On Display Boards
Let's go APE!
H-201
H-202
H-203
R C
H-204
MINE!
H-205
H-206
13
H-207
H-208
RETAIL FOR 10c EA.
720
NEXT
H-209
Order By Number
H-210

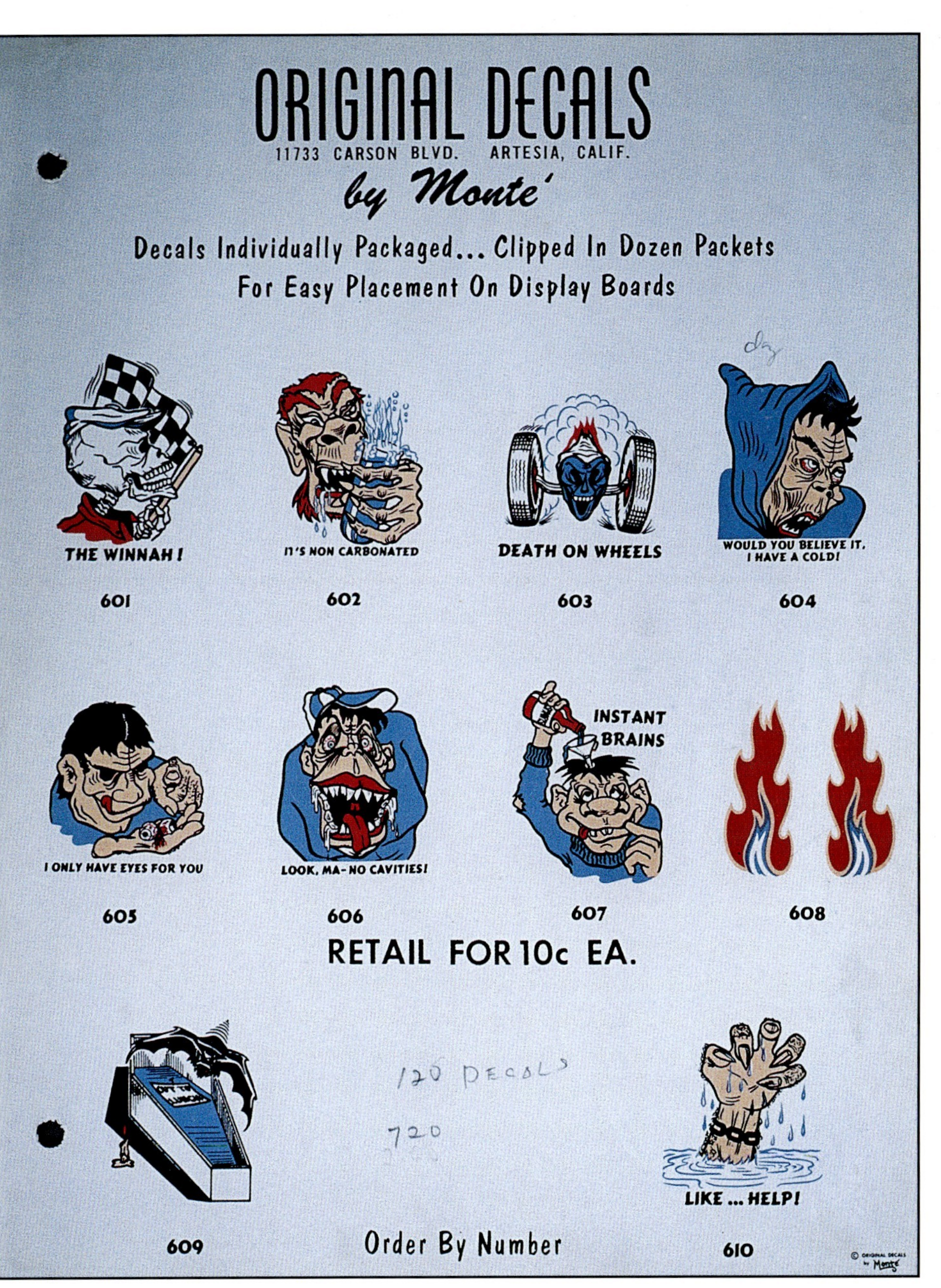
ORIGINAL DECALS
11733 CARSON BLVD. ARTESIA, CALIF.
by Monte'
Decals Individually Packaged... Clipped In Dozen Packets
For Easy Placement On Display Boards
THE WINNAH!
IT'S NON CARBONATED
DEATH ON WHEELS
WOULD YOU BELIEVE IT, I HAVE A COLD!
601
602
603
604
I ONLY HAVE EYES FOR YOU
LOOK, MA-NO CAVITIES!
INSTANT BRAINS
605
606
607
608
RETAIL FOR 10c EA.
120 DECALS
720
LIKE ... HELP!
609
Order By Number
610

All three of these—or variations of them—were picked up by Impko.

Impko sold a variation of this design as "Odd Ball."

The one-eyed, one-horned flying purple people eater, straight from the number one hit of summer, 1958.

Monté's version of the classic bullet-holed flaming skull.

There really was a fascination with beheading in the 50s. Monté made his contribution.

There's a real beatnik feel to this design—or maybe it's just the drum that gives that impression. Very cool image.

Monté evidently dug the outer space thing in a big way.

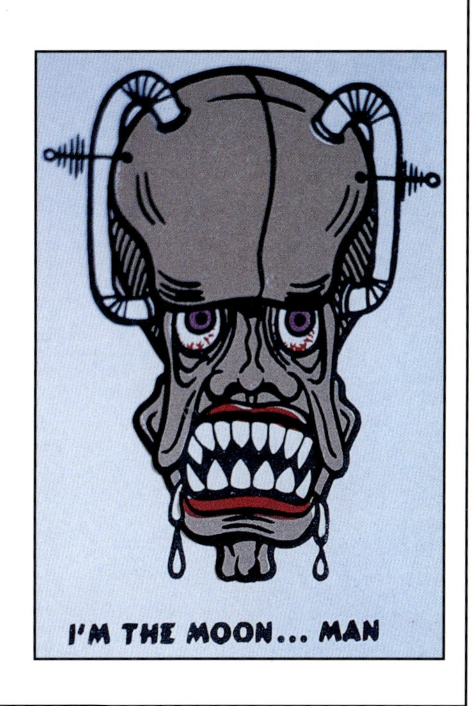

MY MUMMY DONE TOLD ME

THE WINNAH!

13

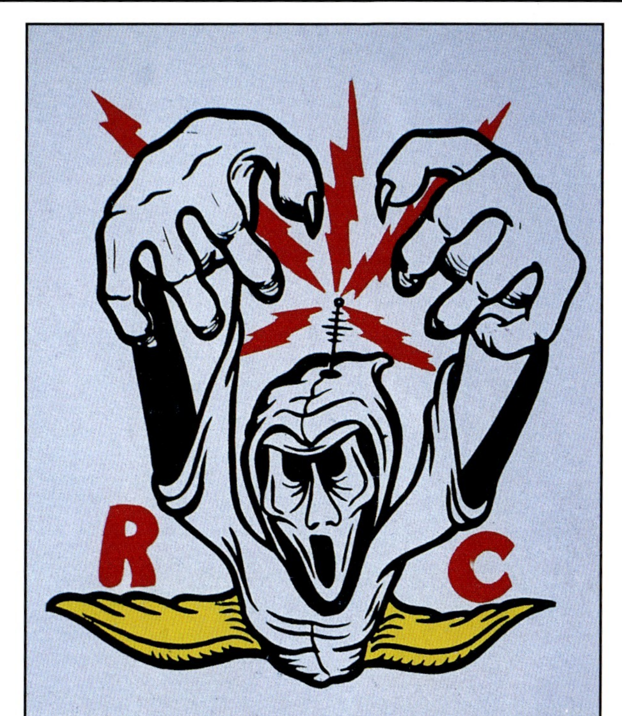
R
C

DEATH ON WHEELS

Chapter 11

Strictly Business

Decals played a major part in commerce by fulfilling their basic role as a way to print on objects that would not fit into a press. They put brand names where they belonged—as on guitars—and provided cheap, dramatic signage, carrying spot and novelty advertising.

Measuring 6"x 9", this 1930s DuPont decal was meant to be window signage in a hardware store, a general store, or anywhere else fine explosives were sold. Dynamite was a common tool for ranchers and farmers, and it was widely available until not too many years ago. In some states it's still easy to get, and even where it's tightly restricted, there are plenty of old-timers who don't consider a pickup truck to be fully equipped unless it's got a couple sticks of dynamite and some blasting caps on board—just in case you've got to move a rock or clear a stump. Very rare decal. $55-$75.

Decals served as the only brand-name identification on Thermaster and Jubilee ice chests, both from the 1950s.

Played by many of country music's leading pedal steel artists, Sho-Bud is to modern steel guitars what Fender is to solid-body electrics. Many pedal steel guitarists who can afford any instrument they want rely on Sho-Bud—and Sho-Bud, to this day, relies on waterslide decals to carry their brand name. Measures 3.25" long, $15-$25.

Old soda-pop vending machine decal—just follow the directions. $10.

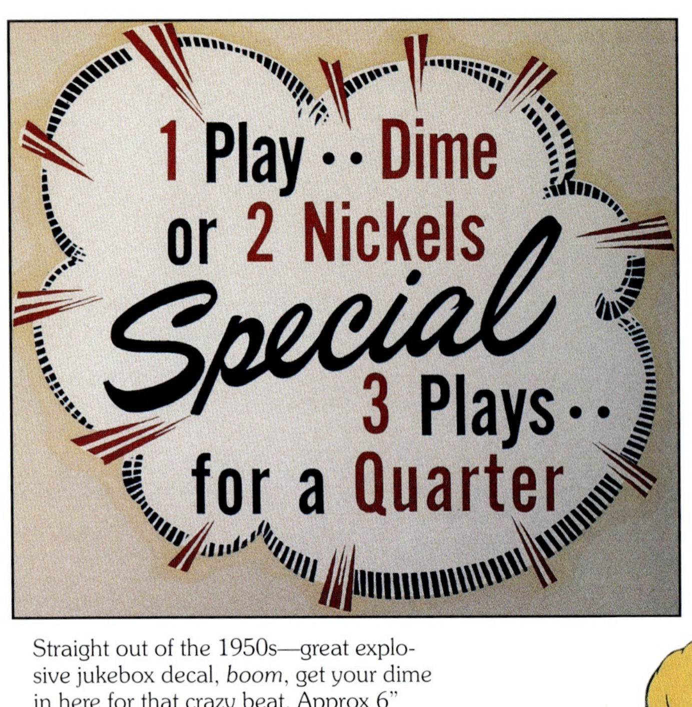

Straight out of the 1950s—great explosive jukebox decal, *boom*, get your dime in here for that crazy beat. Approx 6" across. $10-$15.

Very clean patriotic decal from 1951. Oddly, it was made and sold by the Ozark Gift House in Missouri, which is some distance from any significant naval installations.

Although badly damaged, the little Squirt still gets his point across. 4" tall. If near mint: $15.

Too rarely do you find patriotic art of this caliber. Absolutely magnificent. And the phrase "Citizen Sailor" beats hell out of "Join the Reserves." 4" diameter. $20.

He's Pluto the dog. He's armed with a Thompson submachine gun. And he's receiving radio transmissions with his ass. $15-$20.

Group of Masonic and Shriner's decals—the Ohio map is from a Blue Lodge, the rest are Shriner. The happy face version is pretty clever, using the scimitar as a smile. $5-$10 each.